WATCH YOUR
CHILDREN

WATCH YOUR CHILDREN

Now If He Touched You You Have The
Power To Bring The Delilahs Down

Molly A Phelps

PALMETTO
PUBLISHING
Charleston, SC
www.PalmettoPublishing.com

Copyright © 2024 by Molly A. Phelps

All rights reserved

No portion of this book may be reproduced, stored in a retrieval system, or transmitted in any form by any means–electronic, mechanical, photocopy, recording, or other–except for brief quotations in printed reviews, without prior permission of the author.

Hardcover ISBN: 979-8-8229-2890-9
Paperback ISBN: 979-8-8229-2891-6

Contents

Acknowledgements		vii
Chapter 1	An Unexpected Journey	1
Chapter 2	A Second Chance to Get It Right	4
Chapter 3	Finding Resilience in Silence but in Fear	8
Chapter 4	Childhood Shattered—Innocence Lost to Violation	10
Chapter 5	The Seventh of Seven—Navigating Family Legacy	19
Chapter 6	Lessons from a Fathers' Legacy: Resilience, Nourishment, and Protection	21
Chapter 7	Navigating Parenthood at a Young Age	27
Chapter 8	Nurturing Growth—the Village's Role	29
Chapter 9	If You Train Your Pets, You Should Train Your Children	35
Chapter 10	Learn to Accept Others' Opinions or Advice about Your Child	41
Chapter 11	Prayer Changes Things—Embracing Life at My Prime as a Single Mother	47
Chapter 12	Parents—You Are Your Child's First Role Model	51
Chapter 13	Women Love Men Who Remind Them of Someone as a Father Figure	58
Chapter 14	Barefoot Memories: Navigating Childhood Adversity and the Quest for Belonging	64
Chapter 15	Struggling, Striving, and Thriving: Journey of Resilience as a Wife, Mother, and Family Toward Independence	71

Chapter 16	Growth and Dreams—A Single Mom's Journey	76
Chapter 17	Believe It or Not—Parental Guidance as an Expression of Love	80
Chapter 18	Understanding the Significance of Purpose in Life	86
Chapter 19	A Child's Value and Learning	93
Chapter 20	The Impact of Your Life on Your Children	98
Chapter 21	Reflecting on My Support System	100
Chapter 22	Encouraging Positive Influences for Your Child	101
Chapter 23	A Lesson in Integrity	104
Chapter 24	The Importance of Teaching Your Child—Unveiling Truth	106
Chapter 25	Discovering the Secret to Sustaining Love	109
Chapter 26	Guiding Your Daughter to Embrace Womanhood	112
Chapter 27	Fostering Mutual Respect from Childhood	113

Acknowledgements

I wanted to thank God for my parents, Ruth and Elzie, both for being a beacon of light for me at an early age, especially my father who listened to his mother, Effie, my grandmother, to stay with his children to raise us as best they knew how. At an early age, I didn't share everything with my parents out of fear. After witnessing my parents, who worked to put food on the table, clothes on my back, shoes on my feet, and kept a roof over my head, I am so grateful. By this example, and though I made my bed hard and had to lie in it, I was able to raise my sons gracefully with God's help. I am grateful for those small villages who genuinely cared about me. I am so forever grateful.

CHAPTER 1

An Unexpected Journey

Today is May 28, 2023, and I've long harbored the desire to pen my life story. I am a mother of four sons who found herself thrust into single motherhood when my husband put me out of the family home in July of 1997. At that time, I was twenty-nine, teetering on the edge of my thirties—a period often considered the prime of a woman's life. But where should I start? Well, I embarked on a journey to transform my life by chronicling it in this book and shedding excess weight.

My struggle with weight began in my mid- to late twenties while raising my four sons as a single mom. Interestingly, some individuals who claim to be single aren't truly single; they just aren't married to the person they're romantically involved with. I made a conscious decision to be genuinely single for many years, often imploring God for two things: the means to provide for my children and a better job. I took on multiple jobs to make ends meet, afford a babysitter, or simply earn more money. I was determined that my sons wouldn't call another man "dad."

As my sons grew, the two eldest had already experienced the pain of sporadic contact with their father, and now, they were witnessing my marriage and divorce, making me a single mom once again. I didn't want to further disrupt their childhood with confusion.

During my marriage, there had been a moment when I had to escape through my bedroom window, fearing what might happen if I walked out the front door with our sons. I had once fled to a hotel with my two sons, pregnant with my husbands' child, but I had returned home. On another occasion, I rode a cab to my fathers' senior citizen apartment with my two sons in tow. My father had taken us in and reminded me, "I didn't put you two together, and I won't be the one to break you apart."

I had married the father of my two youngest sons in November of 1992, but our union had lasted a mere five years, the mark of five years in November of the year 1997. He fell into drug use, preventing him from seeing our sons. He even threatened that if he ever got them in his custody, I would never see them again. I shared this information with my attorney, leading to a court order for no contact until he made improvements in his life—a measure taken to protect our family. A church friend informed me that my husband was trading our cars for drugs, which eventually led to our downfall, including the loss of our mortgaged home. We had both worked initially, even running a successful commercial cleaning company at one point. However, our marriage failed, and I found myself once again a single mom without any support, not even child support. I relied on food stamps, welfare checks, and WIC programs at various times to make ends meet. Christmas organizations helped me provide gifts for my sons, and a survivors' disability check from my two eldest sons disabled father, combined with my meager $8.06-per-hour income, helped cover the rent that was due each month before the fifth, under threat of eviction.

While raising my two youngest sons, I navigated public transportation, braving rain, sleet, and snow, often running to catch city buses, waiting on street corners with my boys in tow. My day often felt like an endless journey on those buses, shuttling to work and my parents' house to pick up my sons. My mother walked several miles to retrieve my sons from kindergarten due to their half-day classes while I toiled at work. There were moments when tears welled up crying on my way driving to the second job for additional financial support. My sons needed care, with or without a father in the picture.

CHAPTER 2

A Second Chance to Get It Right

Reflecting on the past, I often think about the fathers of my four sons—two men who left profound marks on our lives. The father of my younger sons passed away tragically after we had been separated for about ten years. Despite our differences, I had reached a place of forgiveness, apologizing for our divorce. His sudden death in a car accident only a few months later left a deep distress with grief.

My heart also holds regret for the lost opportunities with my older sons' father. He battled a long-term illness, enduring dialysis for over twenty-eight years before passing away at sixty-two. We had drifted apart over the years, and my heartfelt regret of not maintaining contact, not allowing us the chance to reconnect and understand each other better. He once proposed to me, but at the time, my heart was set on another path. Sometimes, I wonder about the alternate life we might have shared, with possibly more children even marriage, had circumstances been different.

I have resolved to complete this book, driven by the hope that it would reach and resonate with others. My journey began with a personal challenge—addressing my struggle with weight. This initial step required a significant shift in mindset. I started setting manageable goals, like reading ten pages of a book each day, although I didn't always meet them. Importantly, I stopped making excuses for avoiding exercise.

I've come to understand that neglecting one's health can lead to detrimental consequences. As retirement approached, I turned my focus to financial education, delving into resources like videos on financial freedom and books on money management—including the Bible and other impactful literature.

Interestingly, my second oldest son anticipated this phase in my life. Recognizing my need for guidance as I approached retirement, he gifted me a book on money management. His urging to act "ASAP" was a pivotal moment, emphasizing the urgency of taking control of my life and finances.

My mornings once began routinely with coffee and food. Through my experiences, I've observed a trend among single mothers, me included, of falling into a state of stagnation and complacency. This is particularly true in the challenging context of raising multiple children with minimal involvement from the other parent. The physical and emotional toll often manifests in weight gain and neglected self-care.

To single moms, I want to emphasize the importance of self-care and resilience. Maintain your personal appearance and health. It's essential to keep fit, take care of your nails, hair, skin, and teeth. Remember the attention you paid to these aspects in your teenage or preteen years.

Let that be a reminder that self-care is not just an act of vanity, but an integral part of your overall well-being and confidence. There is always hope, and it's important to never give up on yourself.

To all the single parents out there—mothers, fathers, and those in divorced or separated families—this message is dedicated to you. Parenting, a journey filled with both challenges and joys, demands that we lead not only through our words but also through our actions. Remember, you are the primary role model for your child, a beacon in their lives.

I hold a deep-seated hope that our children will grow to be positive contributors to society, excelling academically from their school years through to college, and eventually embarking on careers that fulfill them. Whether they become entrepreneurs, healthcare professionals, legal experts, athletes, accountants, or follow other paths, our wish is for them to step into a promising future.

Amid these dreams, it's vital not to lose sight of the immediate needs of our children. Keep your home and living spaces clean and organized. This is more than maintaining tidiness; it's about fostering an orderly environment where our children can thrive and develop to their fullest potential.

Managing the myriad responsibilities as a single mother is undoubtedly challenging. It's a journey filled with complexities, but it's important to remember that some men are understanding and accepting of a woman with children, particularly if they are fathers themselves. When mutual love and respect are present, such relationships can be incredibly fulfilling.

Maintaining faith and hope is crucial. If you're reliant on social assistance programs, aim toward self-sufficiency when feasible. In my own journey, I've found strength in prayer and the teachings of the Bible, particularly Matthew 7:7 Ask, and it shall be given you; seek, and ye shall find; knock, and it shall be opened unto you. When I entrusted my needs to

God, focusing on a specific request "One good job, Lord"—it wasn't long before opportunities began to unfold.

For single mothers looking to provide a stable home, explore options like the first-time homebuyer programs. Taking care of your home is important, not just for its physical state but as a stable environment for your children. Whether you plan to sell it later, extract its equity, or purchase another property, treat your home as a valuable asset.

Living as a single parent, I often felt the longing for a partner. During those times, I found solace in walks, using them as opportunities to talk to God and reflect. Embracing your singleness can also be a journey of self-discovery, revealing strengths and capabilities you might not have realized you had.

CHAPTER 3

Finding Resilience in Silence but in Fear

The title of this book, *Watch Your Children*. Reflecting on a woman in the bible called Delilah with the thought *Now If He Touched You—Now You Have the Power to Bring the Delilah's Down*, reflects the story of Delilah and Samson from the Bible. Delilah, given the task of discovering Samson's weakness, portrays a narrative where the misuse of power leads to a man's downfall. However, the underlying moral is also about a woman's ability to destroy a man's life. You must instill in children the importance of proper upbringing for both genders. To my sons, your existence has been my guiding light, propelling me forward despite my past.

Imagine a nine-year-old girl, once hesitant to cross the street, now emboldened to explore the side street of Olney in Indiana. I was never taught to seek permission or ask for anything. I vividly recall the day I ventured to visit one of my best childhood friends, crossing the street confidently to her house. She had a closed-in front porch, and as I knocked on the door that led inside the house, I was abruptly grabbed by the arm. The oldest brother, eighteen at the time, covered my mouth as I screamed! He took me upstairs, where I was molested, violated as a child. Looking back now, I realize he was barely past puberty, but the terror remains etched in my memory.

This continued more than once until it ceased, accompanied by a chilling warning to keep silent, which I did out of fear.

Despite the trauma, I maintained my friendship with her as we transitioned into adulthood. Together, we frequented parties and clubs, and we dated men and one-time-dated brothers. These were the years of my promiscuity, a journey that began at twelve. I became pregnant at fifteen and gave birth to my first son at sixteen. My second son was born when I was seventeen. I initially proposed marriage to him, but later, in my early twenties, he was the one who proposed. I declined, awaiting another man.

The road has been tumultuous, marked by adversity and misguided decisions, but within this turbulence, I found resilience.

CHAPTER 4

Childhood Shattered— Innocence Lost to Violation

Think about when you were a child—an adult, to a child, looks like a giant. Imagine you're standing next to the tallest slide in the playground, one that seems to touch the clouds. Now picture a giant, like someone who could be as tall as that slide. They would be so big that if they walked by, their footsteps might sound like distant thunder, and their heads could be way up in the treetops!

Their hands could be as large as the seat of a swing, and their fingers as long as your whole arm. When they talk, their voice might rumble like the sound of a big truck, deep and loud. Standing next to a giant, you might just reach their knees!

But remember, just like in fairy tales, giants can be friendly and kind. They might be big and strong, but they can have gentle hearts, helping the smaller people in the stories with their great big smiles and even bigger hands. Now when I was nine years old, I was undeveloped and not in puberty at all. I had no breasts, nothing—just a child.

It's natural to question, "Why would a little girl keep returning to this place?" It's important to understand that a child's perspective is different. They might not recognize certain situations as dangerous or harmful, especially in a familiar and seemingly safe environment. My experiences there were a blend of childhood innocence and complex realities. A child doesn't think of molestation as a criminal act punishable under the law when they are not taught. My friend's aunt, and her oldest brothers' aunt also, who worked at a school, had a home where a large cookie jar always seemed inviting. Inside, it was filled with oversized cookies, and she had kindly offered me one during that visit. I had been molested but not during that visit, emphasizing the impact with the thought as a child how one's fear can be like that giant even onto fear of what might happen to me if I said anything. I had the freedom to just walk outside in what seemed like a safe environment. My parents were far from believing that their brave and curious little girl would be sexually violated. I would dismantle the telephone and put it back together, curious to know why the telephone had letters and numbers, anticipating some frequent reaction to my discoveries.

While spending time at my best friend's house, we shared many fond memories. They had a tradition of Sunday dinners, and I often joined them after attending church together. Our adventures included a trip to Kings Island, filled with laughter and excitement. I have cherished memories of her mother baking cakes, generously letting us lick the bowl—a small, yet joyful moment for us. We immersed ourselves in various games like Monopoly, cards, Uno, and outdoor activities such as jump rope, Mother May I, hopscotch, kickball and jacks with marbles, and football.

One recent morning at 1:00 a.m., thoughts of my parents filled my mind, and I pondered a specific memory—or rather, the absence of it. I could not recall a single instance when my father hugged me. This led me to wonder how different things might have been if he had embraced me regularly. In that warmth, I might have found the courage to say, "Daddy, I need to tell you something." This realization underscores the vital importance of open communication between parents and their children. It is essential to be vigilant and attentive (WATCH YOUR CHILDREN!). I will not claim that my parents were bad; they were good people who didn't know how to fully express themselves in raising us. I believe, deep down, if they had known, they would have taken drastic measures to protect their daughter, but fear grasped my very soul as a child, standing taller than my own parents, like that giant. Afraid I would no longer have the freedom to go outside and play, not thinking of the risk, not thinking of how harmful and damaging those actions were to my entire being as I was growing up. As I grew older, I feared adults and being told to respect my elders. Other chosen kin family members had touched me; I have chosen to disclose with forgiveness. Forgiveness is a choice I have made. To stay healed, I had to forgive these people and forgive myself.

Consider yourself as a beautiful garden, a vibrant and valuable symbol of who you are as a woman. Your worth goes beyond superficial attraction; you deserve a partner who recognizes and cherishes your entire being. In a world that often emphasizes physical appearance, it's crucial to understand that true connection involves much more.

The idea of a person seeking their fathers' blessing is an age-old symbol of respect and commitment. It represents a desire for a deep, meaningful connection, not just a fleeting physical attraction. Your partner should be someone who nurtures and supports you, who values you for your intellect, character, dreams, and ambition.

It is important to challenge the notion that men are driven by physical allure at first sight. A fulfilling relationship thrives on mutual respect, understanding, emotional support, and intellectual companionship. A person of true character sees and appreciates the whole person, contributing to a relationship that is enriching, respectful, and loving in every aspect. A man needs a way to think and use his mind to become a man, a provider, a real man with peace of mind.

To all parents, and particularly fathers, I offer this piece of advice: embrace your daughters. The first touch of affection she should know is a hug from her real father. Reflect on the phrase "he gave her away" in the context of a wedding; its significance is profound. It's important to understand that your daughter should not be casually touched by just any man. This can have lasting impacts, potentially leading her to relationships where she might be mistreated verbally and/or physically. Consider carefully the first words out of a child's mouth: "dada." When a child is immorally violated, her or his innocence is taken away.

When children are violated, they can become defiant, it can often mean they are struggling to listen or connect, a form of detachment. It is crucial for a child to feel attached to their parents as they grow, as parents are their primary source of protection and guidance. If a child grows up feeling unprotected or disconnected from their parents, this can lead to their body parts no longer being considered sacred, speaking of a child's violation by an adult. A child can feel unloved even self-esteem issues, seeking approval in the most dangerous places as they grow up to adulthood.

I grew up believing several misconceptions. An important one was that sex is the only way to attract a man. This belief was flawed, because I was never taught the importance of involving a protective figure in my relationships, such as a father, pastor, counselor, or a trusted relative, especially if one's parents are not around. Neither of the men with whom I had children sought my fathers' permission. I am not sure if they were aware they should have, or if my father knew about this custom. Sadly, both fathers of my sons have since passed away. With my ex-husband, we sought counsel from a pastor, but my father was not aware with any details of dating which led to marriage and later divorce, even though he was alive then. I later reached out to my ex-husband to apologize for our divorce, realizing the importance of a father figure for my sons, especially as they faced challenges at school.

Ladies, mothers, and single mothers, it is important to recognize that you are not both parents when raising your children. In my experience, I was solely their mother, not their father. My role was that of a parent, not a friend. Looking back, I regret not fostering a better relationship with the father of my two oldest sons, both for our own understanding and for him to have a deeper connection with his children.

I am immensely proud of all my sons, but I must highlight the accomplishments of my two eldest. They set remarkable examples for their younger brothers. My second oldest son graduated with high honors in high school amongst his senior class and secured a full scholarship to an engineering school, an achievement celebrated with his father at the graduation ceremony during his surprise visit. My eldest son bravely enlisted in the military at eighteen, during the tumultuous period of 9/11. His decision filled me with both pride and concern, especially recalling a coworker's son who tragically did not return from service. Thankfully, my son has built a successful career in the military. Two of my sons became married with children, while the other two remain single. I am proud of each one of them. The two oldest particularly stood out due to their exceptional achievements, which surpassed my wildest expectations. My youngest son has a daughter, my first granddaughter. At her birth, she weighed over nine pounds, and as I looked at her, I promised, "I won't let you down." Her smile in response was priceless. I knew then that I would be authoring this book, and that promise to her was a huge part of my motivation.

As a child, I vividly recall shedding tears on the secluded front porch of our house, shielded by evergreens. I felt a deep sense of being unloved at times. Growing up, I faced relentless bullying and was coerced into fights, despite my aversion to violence. I was ridiculed and ostracized, partly due to my limited wardrobe. Poverty was a stark reality in our family; our pantry was often bare, with beans and potatoes making up the bulk of our meals. However, my father had a talent for cooking anything, especially the fish he caught during our fishing trips. Those outings with my father and brother were not just recreational; they were a respite. We eagerly joined him on visits to relatives' homes because we knew there would be food, and more importantly, I felt a sense of protection in their presence.

Let me share the story of how I was forced out of our home by my then-husband. I remember driving our van, with my children on board, to a doctors' appointment following a work-related injury. Unbeknownst to me, my husband, who was struggling with drug addiction at the time, had tampered with the van's license plates due to the expiration. Previously, a warrant had been issued in my name due to a bounced check I wrote for car repairs. This happened during a phase when my then-husband was frequently withdrawing money for drugs. Although I later settled the payment, my husband assured me that this issue would be settled through our bankruptcy filing, which I naively believed.

One day, while I was driving, the police stopped me for the altered plates and, upon discovering the outstanding warrant, arrested me. I spent a weekend in jail until my husband, lacking the funds for bail, sought help from our church. The church graciously provided the bail money, which was refundable. After my release two days later, I suggested to my husband that we should return the money to the church. His response was explosive and abusive. He ordered me to leave our home. In a state of shock and resolve, I quickly packed what I could and left with our four sons, the oldest being twelve and the youngest just two. As I drove away, I promised myself that I would never let a man put me in such a situation again.

After being forced to leave my home, I temporarily moved in with my mother. She lived in a seven hundred-square-foot senior citizen apartment with just one bedroom. To avoid any attention, as I was not officially allowed to stay there, I used the back door. With my four children in tow, I desperately searched for a new place to live. I explored diverse options, including income-based apartments and Section 8 housing, and even reached out to Habitat for Humanity. However, my efforts was hindered by an eviction on my record, a result of my husband's leaving our previous apartment without paying the last months' rent. As a newlywed I was solely dependent on him.

The situation was dire. My parents were ill, and my siblings, all married, had their own responsibilities. In this time of need, my sister stepped in as a lifesaver. She agreed to cosign for a two-bedroom apartment. I am eternally grateful for her support, as it provided a stable home for me and my sons. Determined to improve our situation and become independent of social assistance programs, I pursued a second job, driven by a relentless will to make it on my own.

In life, certain individuals function as "bridges," divinely positioned to guide us toward our destiny. They play a crucial role, often arriving at pivotal moments. While working at the hospital, I took a seasonal job with the Postal Service. There, I encountered a man by the time clock. He was charming and flirtatious, which was flattering, particularly as a young mother of four. He was well-established in his career, a trait I found appealing.

However, I was still legally married, though on the path to divorce, and was not seeking a new relationship. My priority was my children's well-being. This employees' presence served as a catalyst for a different kind of inspiration. Instead of pursuing a romantic involvement, I saw an opportunity for professional growth. I sought a stable, long-term career at the Postal Service, a decision that profoundly changed my life.

This job enabled me to provide better for my sons. We lived in the apartment for six years, during which time I worked diligently to build credit. Eventually, this effort paid off, allowing me to purchase a home in a good neighborhood. This home wasn't just a structure; it was a testament to resilience, independence, and the power of making strategic life choices.

CHAPTER 5

The Seventh of Seven– Navigating Family Legacy

Many days, I have felt like the black sheep, but I know my family loved me.

Today, I was reflecting on my siblings. I am the seventh child, born on the twenty-seventh day of the month (September) in the year 1967, the beginning part of the word Sept means the number seven but on the Gregorian calendar it's the ninth month. I was my parents' last child, and our family consisted of four boys and two girls. Sadly, my mother had another child who passed away. All my siblings were able to marry except one who had disabilities. Three of my brothers married the mothers of their children, while one of my brothers passed away at the age of forty-one. My sister married at the age of seventeen and has been with her husband, with whom she has children, for over forty-eight years now. My sister and my two brothers are still married, but not me. I have been married only once, in less than five years, and both of my children's fathers passed away. I have often questioned myself. I have a darker complexion than the rest of my family, as everyone else is light skinned. I have wondered why this happened to me. Was it a punishment from God? Did someone cast negative words upon me? Did I wrong someone so severely that they wished for me to be a single parent struggling? I have had many questions on my mind.

My father was the backbone of our family, and he had a deep love for us.

CHAPTER 6

Lessons from a Fathers' Legacy: Resilience, Nourishment, and Protection

During my childhood, my brother and I would eagerly watch as our father backed his car out of the driveway. We would sprint toward him, shouting to catch up and join him in the car. Fishing was one of my fathers' favorite pastimes, and I have fond memories of our aunts, uncles, and cousins accompanying us to pick field greens, known as poke salad. I recall watching my father harvest heads of cabbage from a nearby farm. To support our family, my father collected copper, aluminum cans, and newspapers to exchange for cash. We frequently visited our relatives' homes, and one of my aunts always had a delightful spread of soul food ready for us. We would enjoy meals at all their houses. I also witnessed my father salvaging greens from a supermarket dumpster. He once told me that the grocery store had discarded an entire ham, and we enjoyed that unexpected find as well. We made the most of every opportunity to access food; although we faced financial hardships and had limited resources.

Let me share something truly special about all of this. My father was our family's primary provider. He would often take us to visit cousins and relatives, and in their company, I always felt a warm sense of belonging. What made it even more remarkable was watching my father cook for us. He proudly mentioned that he had been a chef for a hotel for nineteen years. As a single mother, I was able to apply what I had learned from observing my fathers' culinary skills to cook for my own sons. I began cooking for myself at the tender age of ten or eleven. I would meticulously peel and cut potatoes into French fry style, heat up the pan with oil on our gas stove, and ignite the fire to prepare my meals. My brother and I would playfully act like robots while eating what our father prepared and cooked, using the mealtime as a source of energy. Writing about these memories brings tears to my eyes, especially when I think about my brother. Every Thursday, my father received his paycheck, and he would bring home bags of groceries. The food never lasts long due to limited resources. The food was perishable, and nonperishable, which needed to be carefully in preparation cooked. He had to hide food to prevent us from devouring it all. Although the food was rationed due to a large family, we always had a steady supply of potatoes, beans, and sugar.

Let me share how incredibly special it was to go fishing with my father—it was truly awesome! I would take a stick, tie a fishing string to the stick, and attach a hook from my father's fishing toolbox. After baiting it with a worm, I would cast my line and catch a fish. My father would treat us to potato chips and soda (pop). He always had bologna, cheese, and crackers in hand. Though my father drank, he never did so excessively while we were in the car with him.

We never ventured too close to the water during our fishing trips; we knew the importance of staying safe and avoiding the risk of drowning. Sadly, we had a neighbor up the street who met such a tragic fate while swimming in the same lake my father took us to. It was a sobering reminder of the dangers of water.

In our home, my father kept a sawed-off shotgun securely locked in his bedroom closet, and all of us kids knew never to touch that gun.

In all that time, I never told my father about the sexual violation when I was child, out of fear.

WATCH YOUR CHILDREN! I've accessed child abuse statistics from the Indiana Center for The Prevention of Youth Abuse, and the findings are deeply troubling. According to the statistics, one out of every four girls experience sexual abuse before they reach the age of eighteen. I strongly encourage you to review these statistics for yourselves. I encourage you to read it for yourself. It also says that women who report childhood rape have an alarming triple likelihood to become pregnant before eighteen years of age. I did. Ninety percent of abusers are people children know, love and trust. I did. (WATCH YOUR CHILDREN.)

In our church, we had a godmother known as Big Mama. I was a regular attendee, especially while raising my first two sons. The church's elder women would candidly share insights about our children and offer guidance on raising them. Though some parents were reluctant to listen, they spoke their truths regardless. Big Mama once advised, "Never let your children go places you haven't been." This meant not sending my children somewhere without my presence. This advice led me to a rule: I realized not to allow my children to sleep over some other child's home unless the invitation was extended to me, and I asked the question on their behalf: When children are asked to spend the night at someone house, The real question: "Do you know the family?" Have you visited their home? Have you spoken with their parents? Do you know who else will be around your child? What are their plans during your child's stay? Is it acceptable for you to make an unexpected visit?

When I moved to a suburban area, there were instances of parents taking my youngest sons for sleepovers without my consent. It is important to recognize that not all parents share your parenting style. So, parents, please be respectful and do not simply take a child's word for it.

Children often develop a sense of entitlement regarding their parents' home, evident in phrases like "my room," "my food," "my stuff," "my house," and so on. As parents, it is important to teach children to ask permission for anything they need, except for essentials like water. I observed this in my own family. My eldest sons, who were nine to ten years older than their younger siblings, grew up with a respectful fear of overstepping boundaries with me. They always asked before doing something. In contrast, my younger sons were much like I was as a child—they had the freedom to go outside and play with friends without asking for permission. I thought the safety of living in the suburbs in a good neighborhood was enough, but it was not. Although we thankfully had no incidents of molestation, the two youngest struggled academically in school and there were times I did not feel the need to discipline, at times not necessarily for the sake of just acting normally as children. As a single mother working hard to maintain our home, I always emphasized to them the importance of speaking up if someone touched them inappropriately, regardless of any threats.

Reflecting on my journey through my late twenties, thirties, forties, and now well into my fifties, I realize the challenges of raising my sons alone. There was no man in my life by choice, a decision made to protect my sons unless their fathers had chosen to be a part of their lives.

Growing up, house parties were common in my neighborhood. I never spent much time in front of the mirror or focused on my appearance, yet I had an unacknowledged attractiveness. In fact, I was warned not to attend school on my last day or face being beaten up due to jealous behaviors associated from others. Around the age of twelve or thirteen, I remember attending one of these house parties with a friend. At the party, a boy who had a strong liking for me stayed close by my side throughout the evening. When another guy wanted to dance with me, the boy who liked me would not allow it. This led to a confrontation where the other guy punched him, sending him through a door. In the chaos that ensued, my friend quickly grabbed my arm, urging, "We got to get out of here!" Moments later, we heard gunshots while running. Now later in life I could not help but think about the challenges that arise when raising children without boundaries or rules. It reminded me of my own youth when I used to walk to my friends' houses at the tender ages between thirteen and fourteen. I would cover several miles to visit them, just as I did with all the other childhood friends. It was during those times that her mother would frequently leave to spend the weekends with her boyfriend, leaving my friend in charge of her younger sisters. My friend and I were about the same age, and unfortunately, she faced the consequences of this situation. She became pregnant at the age of thirteen and had two children by the time she turned fifteen years old.

Nowadays, a teenager's thoughts are consumed by her hair, her shape, her wardrobe, and her footwear and adorning nails. I was no exception; these were my primary concerns at the time. However, I must also mention that back then, our home had limited food, almost none to speak of. It was during this period that I began to realize the importance of having enough to eat, especially when I saw my relatives and friends had access to ample food. It may sound a bit unusual, but it all ties into my journey. You see, I eventually got married, and initially, my husband excelled in securing employment and even ventured into starting his own business. I entrusted my earnings to him to provide for our family, and things were going well during that phase.

CHAPTER 7

Navigating Parenthood at a Young Age

From what I recall, I was about ten when I started braiding hair, mastering both simple and French braids without any formal instruction. My skills became well known in my neighborhood, especially after I styled a friend's hair in high school, emulating the look of Patrice Rushen. This passion led me to enroll in beauty college, where I excelled both in practical skills and academics. I even started cutting my first two sons' hair, giving them stylish bald fades. My journey back to school started when I was seventeen, already expecting my second child. I made the decision at a friend's apartment; despite the skepticism I faced, I was determined. I remember her mother questioning my choice, but I was undeterred.

However, things changed when I married. My husband asked me to take a leave of absence from college to assist him with his business. During this time, I received news that the beauty school had gone bankrupt. Overwhelmed with marital challenges, I never managed to return to school and complete my education. As my marriage faced increasing difficulties, my dreams and aspirations seemed to drift further away. The most valuable advice I can offer to anyone pursuing their dreams or career is to consider the impact of marriage on your goals.

The path was not easy. I had to rely on city buses for transportation, followed by a two-mile walk, often crossing railroad tracks pregnant walking to high school. One day, while waiting for a train, I encountered another student who, in haste, contemplated crossing under the moving train. I advised against it, and thankfully, he heeded my warning. This experience underscored the importance of patience and safety, values I carried with me as I navigated the challenges of pursuing education as a young, expectant mother.

At fifteen, during my first pregnancy, I remember sitting on my parents' back porch, gazing skyward, and challenging God with my words: "You can't even help me." Surprisingly, help came in an unexpected form. My brother and his family arrived in their station wagon, offering me a ride. If they had mentioned church, I would likely have declined, as I wasn't inclined toward religious settings then.

It seemed like a simple invitation, but I believe there was more to it. Perhaps God understood my needs better than I did and chose that moment to reach out, not through a church invitation, but through a simple, inclusive gesture from my family. This experience made me reflect on the mysterious ways in which support and guidance can manifest in our lives.

CHAPTER 8

Nurturing Growth—the Village's Role

Reflecting on my journey as a teenager transitioning into motherhood, I recall the period when I started attending church regularly, thanks to my brother and his family, who took me in. This new chapter of my life was marked by discipline and a shift toward a cleaner lifestyle—what some might consider strictness or austerity. My brother, protective and perhaps a bit stern, had reservations about my baby's father contacting me. He insisted I adhere to certain rules, ones I found too rigid and hard to align with.

The situation escalated when the pastor, misunderstanding my intentions, thought I was seeking autonomy in a way that contradicted the church's principles. This misunderstanding led to my eventual departure from both the church and my brother's home, a challenging moment that coincided with the birth of my first child, only days old. This experience taught me about the complexities of seeking support and the importance of mutual understanding in the communities that raise us.

There was a time when I faced untrue accusations from a church member, who claimed I was involved with a man outside the church. This was not the case; appreciating someone doesn't imply a romantic relationship. Yet I noticed a troubling pattern: when I took care of my appearance, some labeled me negatively, as if self-care was synonymous with seeking male attention. This unfair judgment led me to develop an inferiority complex, constantly feeling scrutinized and misunderstood.

Struggling with these perceptions, I gained a significant amount of weight, and interestingly, no one seemed to mind. But as soon as I lost weight, the accusations resurfaced. This experience highlighted a double standard within my community, where personal health and self-improvement efforts were misinterpreted and judged.

I often pondered the teachings of love and respect between men and women in the scriptures. Isn't it natural to desire companionship and maintain one's health and appearance? Yet, when I exercised at the gym for my well-being, it was misconstrued as seeking attention.

Despite these challenges, the experience was profoundly educational. We were encouraged to prepare and present our own meditations to the congregation, sharing our personal interpretations of the scriptures. This process was not just informative, but also therapeutic.

The discipline I gained from studying the Bible played a significant role in my self-awareness and understanding of proper conduct and righteous living. Although there were times when I strayed from these teachings, I eventually returned to the church with both of my children. This marked the beginning of a nineteen-year journey as a member, a period filled with growth, learning, and self-discovery.

Through these trials, I've come to understand that while people may have good intentions, it is ultimately God who knows us best. We all have a fundamental need for companionship and recognition, which doesn't necessitate compromising our values or integrity. This journey has taught me the importance of self-love and the courage to pursue personal well-being, irrespective of others' misjudgments.

In my early twenties, I joined a gym to maintain my fitness. Interestingly, my then-boyfriend, who later became my husband, was so concerned about my gym membership that he even sought the church attorney's help. Those actions only discouraged me. Throughout our marriage, I emphasized the importance of not neglecting our health, especially as I noticed a hundred-pound weight gain on my part. But my concerns were met with indifference, summed up in his words: "You're tripping."

This experience taught me a crucial lesson about relationships: if you enter a marriage loving someone at a certain state, it is important to encourage and support each other's well-being. In my case, the lack of support contributed to our marriages' downfall.

I want to emphasize to all women the importance of self-care. It is about honoring the body and soul that God has given you, irrespective of a man's presence in your life. If someone does come along who wants to be with you, you should not have to rush to change yourself. Maintain your health and appearance for yourself first. It is not just about looking good for others but feeling good for yourself. As the saying goes, "How do you like them apples?"—it is about loving and accepting yourself first and foremost.

I once collaborated with a woman who always covered her hair, and it intrigued me. My own hair was usually worn down, and I initially thought her choice was a religious practice. However, I learned that she covered her hair as a symbol of her grief, not due to religious reasons. It made me realize that in some cultures and religions, women do cover their hair, sometimes in mourning and sometimes as a part of their faith.

I felt a deep connection with her, understanding her sense of loss more than she might have realized. She was a woman without a partner's love, and her only daughter was grown and married. In a heartfelt moment, she shared with me that she was praying for me and for the souls of aborted babies. Her insight into the world's sorrows seemed profound.

Moved by her expression of sorrow and the depth of her understanding, I decided to cover my hair as well. It was not just a gesture of solidarity with her; I was also grieving. It was my way of externally manifesting the internal grief that I, too, was experiencing.

During a particularly difficult phase in my life, I found myself battling depression. This struggle deeply affected my self-image, especially as I dealt with obesity. The weight gain began in my mid to late twenties and has been a constant challenge, with my weight lingering above two hundred pounds for several years.

Reflecting, I was around 135 pounds when I first met the father of my first son. By the time I met my husband, my weight fluctuated between 150 to 165 pounds, which I felt was ideal for me. However, my husband once expressed that if I lost weight, I might leave him. Ironically, my motivation for attending the gym was twofold: to maintain my own sense of desirability and to keep my marriage intact.

This period of my life highlighted the complex relationship between self-worth, physical appearance, and how others' perceptions and fears can profoundly impact our actions and self-image.

In my early preteens, while in the kitchen with my father, he shared a piece of advice that stayed with me. He believed that to find a good man, I would need to venture far south, almost to an unimaginable extent. In essence, he was suggesting, "Don't settle for anyone here; go south to meet your future husband." At that time, thoughts of boyfriends or relationships were far from my mind.

During my pregnancy, a relative suggested to my mother that I should have an abortion. My mother adamantly opposed this, drawing from her own regretful experience of having had an abortion with her first child. She advised my sister to ensure I never went through with an abortion.

My father's perspective on relationships and marriage was traditional. He believed that a man interested in his daughter should seek his permission, especially for marriage. This tradition was not followed in my case. I remember a schoolmate visiting me once; my father was in his favorite spot in the backyard. I cannot recall if the schoolmate ever approached him, but that instance stands out as a reminder of the values and expectations my father held.

Reflecting on my family background, I acknowledge that my parents did their best, though perhaps they were not fully equipped to raise us in certain aspects. My sister's experience was quite different from mine. She became pregnant at fourteen and married the father of her children, who respectfully asked for my father's permission, as I understand. They started their life together both at a young age and have been together for over forty-eight years. My brothers, too, have maintained stable marriages with the women they had children with. My path, in contrast, diverged from this pattern, highlighting the unique and varied journeys we all navigate in life.

It is crucial to teach children about personal safety. They should be encouraged to communicate openly if anyone touches them inappropriately, specifying who it was and what happened. This open line of communication is essential for their protection and well-being.

Responsibility is another key aspect of child-rearing. Children should be taught to seek permission for their actions. In my own experience, the lack of this requirement led to a traumatic incident. I left my house without notifying anyone, which unfortunately resulted in an encounter where I was molested. The assailant attempted to further violate me, and I often think that if his intentions had been fully realized, my life could have been drastically different. This personal story underscores the importance of vigilance and communication in parenting.

CHAPTER 9

If You Train Your Pets, You Should Train Your Children

Let us circle back to that enchanting garden. One Christmas, I surprised my son with a gift he would never forget—a German shepherd puppy, just eight weeks old, tiny enough to nestle into my purse. You might wonder, what does a picturesque garden have to do with a puppy? The story unfolds with each line.

My childhood was filled with the constant presence of pets. In particular, two German shepherds were a fixture in our backyard, albeit sadly chained. A vivid memory that lingers is a frightening encounter with one of them when I was about nine. That experience, unforgettable and intense, shaped my perspective on pets.

In keeping with this lifelong connection to dogs, I decided to gift one of my sons with his own canine companion. In a nod to a character, we both cherished, we named her Samantha, inspired by the brave and loyal dog from *I Am Legend*, accompanying as Will Smith's star host.

German shepherd dogs are renowned for their intelligence. Often serving as K-9 units in police departments, these dogs are lauded for their smarts rather than any innate viciousness. Their formidable appearance, however, can be intimidating to many.

Samantha, our German Shepherd, was no exception. She had a discerning nature, warm to those she favored. My sons had friends who would visit, and while some were greeted with enthusiasm, Samantha was selective. One friend found favor with her, able to stroke her as one would a cat, a privilege she did not extend to everyone.

An incident while walking Samantha illustrated her discerning nature vividly. We encountered a neighbor outside. While Samantha sat calmly, the neighbor reached out to pet her without asking. To my surprise and shock, Samantha snapped at her. This incident underscored the importance of respecting a dog's space, something the neighbor had previously not considered.

This experience with Samantha leads to a broader reflection. Shouldn't we aim to instill in our children the same discernment and self-awareness? I am using my dog as an example that no one should be able to touch a child inappropriately and in this case the neighbor did nothing wrong nor Samantha. Without fear children should be free to express themselves when they are violated or feel threatened. Or in cases where a couple decides to date in high hopes of possibly marriage more serious and that woman or man decides not to be touched considered to be inappropriate to them and expresses herself or himself in real contempt. Like Samantha, they should learn to interact with the world around them thoughtfully and confidently.

In today's society, fashion choices often spark complex conversations about perception and respect. It's important to recognize that clothing can be a form of self-expression, yet it can also inadvertently invite unwarranted assumptions. The responsibility for respectful interaction, however, always lies with the observer, not the person being observed.

It's crucial to remember that we live in a diverse world where women's choices, including their attire, reflect their personal style and autonomy. Judging someone solely based on their appearance reduces their complexity as an individual. As we navigate through this world of diverse women and men, fostering a culture of respect and understanding becomes paramount.

The trauma of child molestation has profound and complex effects, akin to placing a child in a situation as overwhelming and dangerous as driving a car—it's a burden too heavy and inappropriate for their age. Such experiences can lead to a myriad of behavioral changes, including defiance and challenges in adhering to parental guidance.

It's crucial to understand that these behavioral shifts may be a cry for help rather than mere acts of rebellion. A sudden change in attitude, particularly an increased defiance or curiosity about sexual matters, can sometimes be an indicator of underlying distress. This doesn't necessarily mean they are engaging in sexual activities, but it could signify that the child is processing something they don't fully understand or that has harmed them.

In these situations, a compassionate and supportive approach is essential. Parents and guardians should seek professional guidance to ensure the child receives the appropriate care and support to heal and navigate these challenges.

Guidelines for Teaching Children Essential Life Skills

1. Financial Literacy: Start teaching children about money management from an early age. This includes understanding the value of money and the basics of saving.
2. Household Chores: Encourage children to participate in household chores. This teaches responsibility and contributes to a sense of family teamwork.
3. Understanding Consequences: Educate children about the concept of consequences for actions, both positive and negative. This helps them understand the impact of their choices.
4. Politeness and Gratitude: Emphasize the importance of saying "please" and "thank you." Learning to express gratitude is a valuable life lesson.
5. Outdoor Play: Encourage children to play outside. It is important for their physical and mental health. Parents should actively engage in this time, supervising and participating when possible.
6. Sleepovers: Exercise caution with sleepovers at other people's homes. It is important to know the environment and the adults involved. Always prioritize your child's safety and comfort.
7. Media Consumption: Be mindful of the content children are exposed to on television, opt for educational shows and ensure that the messages are positive and age appropriate. Not all cartoons and shows are beneficial for children.

Taking your children on vacation is a priceless experience. I vividly recall a trip to Florida with my sister, my niece, and her son, who was six at the time. We embarked on an exciting journey to Walt Disney World, staying in a resort and exploring three out of the four parks, including the vibrant city walk.

The most poignant moment came at Magic Kingdom. Surrounded by the joy and laughter of families, I found myself overwhelmed with emotion and tears streamed down my face. These tears were a mix of joy and a touch of regret. As a single mom, I had always dreamed of bringing my own sons to this magical place. Despite the financial challenges and the sizeable refund checks and a well-paying job I later secured, I never made this dream a reality. At that moment, I realized the significance of such experiences in creating lasting memories.

This journey was more than just a vacation; it was a reflection on missed opportunities and the importance of seizing the moment to make lasting memories with loved ones.

Engaging in meaningful activities with children can significantly boost their self-esteem and set a foundation for success later in life. Here are some key practices:

1. Teaching Moral Values: Introduce children to the Ten Commandments or similar ethical guidelines. This helps inculcate a strong moral compass.
2. Quiet Time: Encourage periods of quiet time for reflection or reading. This helps children learn the value of stillness and introspection.
3. Prayer Time: If your family is religious, dedicating time to prayer can instill a sense of spiritual grounding and community.

4. Playtime: Ensure children have time for play. This is crucial for their creative and social development.
5. Education on Personal Boundaries: Instruct children about bodily autonomy and the importance of personal boundaries, including the appropriate times to touch their private parts, like during bathing.
6. Individual Attention: If you have multiple children, spend one-on-one time with each. This could be a special dinner or attending a sports game together. It shows each child they are valued individually.
7. Family Meals: Encourage family dinners. This shared time strengthens family bonds and provides a platform for open communication.
8. Positive Communication: Avoid speaking negatively about any absent parent. Children process information differently than adults, and negative remarks can impact their emotional wellbeing.

CHAPTER 10

Learn to Accept Others' Opinions or Advice about Your Child

No matter how parents view themselves, their child invariably sees them as Mom or Dad—not as good or bad, just as their parent. This perspective underscores why one parent should never speak ill of the other in front of or to the child. Negative comments can foster resentment and anger as the child grows. This principle highlights the value of experienced individuals guiding those who are newer to parenting. In my experience, wise advice from older women in my church community, such as refrain from speaking negatively about an absent father, was invaluable. When my children asked about their father, I maintained neutrality, knowing that negative remarks could not only harm their perception of him but also affect their overall well-being and success. This approach nurtures a healthy environment for the child's growth, free from unnecessary emotional burdens.

For those of us with children and homes with multiple rooms, an important piece of advice I learned from a coworker is about the setup of a bedroom. Specifically, it's beneficial not to have a television in a child's bedroom. This approach encourages family bonding and healthier habits. For instance, my coworker once called her daughter, who was isolated upstairs in her bedroom, to come down to the family room and watch TV together. This small change can have a significant impact. It is a reminder that each room has its purpose. Promoting shared activities, like watching TV in a shared area, fosters family togetherness and a more organized home environment.

Growing up, I was taught the importance of respecting elders. However, it led me to ponder: Does "elder" refer to someone just because they are older, like an eighteen-year-old, or does it exclude those who mistreat us? These reflections are part of my long journey in writing, a journey that brought me to a pivotal realization: I needed to change my life. Part of this transformation involved completing this book, hoping it might guide someone to help a child or children.

I began walking to improve my physical health, discipline, and overall wellness. Alongside this, I altered my diet. Reflecting on my early twenties, I remember exercising rigorously, doing sit-ups with my feet partly under my mom's couch. Back then, anxiety made me pace, but I never turned to food for comfort. That habit developed later.

To further my personal growth, I started listening to positive videos about finance and self-improvement. Reading inspirational books also became a part of my routine. These changes rekindled my passion for authoring this book.

I share my journey in the hope that it inspires you to continue reading and discover your own unique gift to offer the world. People need the wisdom and experiences we share.

One day, a friend from church pointed out something to me: "Molly, you've never really focused on taking care of yourself." This comment came when I was in my twenties, a time when I was juggling two jobs and raising four children. My friend noticed I did not frequent nail salons or beauty parlors, nor did I indulge in skincare routines. She was right. My children were my foremost priority, and personal luxuries took a backseat.

During this phase, as I regularly attended church; our community supported me. We received clothes, shoes, and even furniture. I lived modestly in half of a double house with extremely low rent. Growing up with limited means, I was accustomed to a simple life. My rare splurges on new purses or clothes were usually for special occasions.

Even after getting married, my spending habits did not change much. I did not accumulate many purses, clothes, or shoes. Reflecting on this, I realize that I had naturally become a person who valued nonmaterialistic aspects of life more deeply.

Growing up, I had a wardrobe that was quite limited. My mother, doing her best, often shopped at Goodwill and the Salvation Army to provide for our clothing needs. Unlike many, I did not frequent shopping malls or chase designer labels, a habit that continued even when I started working.

As a young teen, around twelve or thirteen, I found a way to add a personal touch to my wardrobe. I used to babysit for my siblings, earning some money in return. With the money my sister gave me, I remember taking the bus downtown to shop for clothes and boots. This small act of independence was thrilling. I carefully selected a pair of nice pants and a top, along with a pair of boots made of leather and suede. These shopping trips were more than about clothes; they were about making choices for myself, and I truly cherished that experience.

As a young girl, I have vivid memories of my mother or sister taking care of my hair. They used a hot comb, also known as a pressing comb, to straighten my hair. On days when we did not press my hair, my sister would simply use a comb or brush, a bit of oil, and water to manage it. These moments were more than about hair care; they were bonding experiences and a part of our daily life.

My sister faced significant challenges early on. She became pregnant at the tender age of fourteen, and her boyfriend at the time, who was three years older, was the father of my niece and nephew. Due to our parents' concerns about managing additional responsibilities, my sister had to leave home. Despite these early hardships, my sister, and her boyfriend, united by their situation, got married. Impressively, they have been together for over forty-seven years, having never separated or divorced. Their journey stands as a testament to resilience and commitment, even in the face of daunting challenges.

Growing up, I observed my mother not prioritizing her own self-care, a habit I inadvertently adopted. As I matured, I realized the need to change this pattern. My sister, in contrast, has always been conscientious about her self-care, maintaining her weight, grooming her eyebrows, and using a touch of makeup. I used to wear makeup regularly but gradually stopped, even though I still own some.

Our family environment was often tense due to the frequent arguments between my parents. These disputes were not about money, but other issues. Job opportunities for Black people during that time were limited, as I recall. My father worked as a janitor and received his paycheck every Thursday. My mother held jobs as a nurses' aide at a local nursing home and worked at a laundry service. However, for reasons unknown to me, she eventually stopped working there.

Later, she stayed home for a while before taking a job at a mall. She then worked downtown, cleaning office buildings, until she was sixty-two, retiring to collect social security. These experiences shaped my understanding of work, responsibility, and the importance of self-care, influencing my journey toward personal development and understanding my heritages' impact on my family's opportunities and challenges.

When I secured a well-paying job with the government at the age of thirty-four, my first ambition was to buy a house. This goal was a significant step for me, a single mother raising four sons. I had made a conscious decision at twenty-nine to raise my children without a man in our lives, following the absence of their father. I believed that if their father was not present, no other man should be in our home. The only male influences I allowed were men from our church, who provided a positive presence.

My eldest son enlisted in the military at eighteen and built a career there. My second son excelled academically, earning a full scholarship to a private high school, then to an engineering college, and eventually to graduate school. They both played a crucial role in helping with their younger brothers, especially when I worked multiple jobs to support us.

I managed to have a house built and moved us to the suburbs. Our home was part of a rapidly constructed community known as "cookie cutter homes" due to their similar designs. It was a nice area, and still is, but maintaining it was a constant struggle. There were times I almost lost our home and had to resort to filing for bankruptcy to avoid eviction.

These experiences were challenging, but they taught me resilience and the value of perseverance. Despite the hardships, I was determined to provide a stable and loving home for my sons.

I vividly recall a particularly challenging time when I had initiated bankruptcy proceedings but hadn't completed the payment to file. On a bitterly cold, snowy day, with my sons safe and warm at home, I faced a daunting reality. I called the mortgage company to inquire about the foreclosure and learned, to my dismay, that a sheriff's sale of our home was scheduled to start the very next day.

Panicked, I immediately contacted my attorney. She urgently advised me to come to her office right away to finalize the bankruptcy filing and halt the foreclosure process. Acting swiftly, I followed her guidance, a decision that prevented us from losing our home.

This period was marked by financial struggles, compounded by the challenges of raising my sons without their father's presence. The difficulties in paying bills and managing household expenses were significant, but these experiences also highlighted my determination and resilience in ensuring stability and security for my family.

CHAPTER 11

Prayer Changes Things—Embracing Life at My Prime as a Single Mother

For over twenty years, I have resided at my current address, raising four sons single-handedly. To the single mothers and fathers reading this, I extend my heartfelt gratitude. I remember once reading a detailed check to God, laying out precisely what I needed. It reminds me of a verse in the King James Bible: "Now unto Him that is able to do exceedingly abundantly above all that we ask or think, according to the power that worketh in us." It is essential to ask God explicitly for your desires. A minister echoed this as I watched on television, who advocated for writing letters to God.

Following my divorce, I found solace and strength in prayer, drawing nearer to God during this challenging phase. In times of deep distress, I discovered the true essence of prayer. While I was employed at the hospital. A minister had graciously stated while listening to his sermon gave the advice to many of his viewers to write a letter to God. In doing so I decided to read my earnings/check to God in detail on how much was printed such as taxes, insurances, and wages etc. as a gesture of faith and gratitude."

Earning just $8.06 an hour, I faced the challenge of raising four sons alone. We made do in a modest two-bedroom apartment, conveniently close to my job, to which I could walk. My two older sons stepped up, caring for their younger siblings while I juggled work and a second job. We relied on food stamps for a while, but I aspired for more than a life dependent on social programs. I was aware of housing assistance available for single mothers, offering minimal to no rent, but I knew such programs had their limits. They do not pave the way to homeownership or allow for continued assistance once you secure a well-paying job or increase your income. I was determined to break free from these constraints.

I have come to understand something profound about God and personal desires. When longing for a companion, if the intention is pure, God often fulfills these heartfelt desires. This is not about sin; it's about the natural yearning of a woman to love and be loved by a man. As I have aged, I've realized my lack of education in respecting a partner. My ex-husband and I rarely argued, not because of mutual understanding, but because I chose not to retaliate. "Big Mama," a wise figure in my church, once told me that it takes two to create fuss. Although I never talked back during my marriage, I was influenced by the bitterness and jealousy of others around me. Looking back, I see that there was room for improvement. I was not guided on how to be a submissive, godly woman in a relationship, which I now view as important.

I have come to understand that some people act as bridges, guiding us to where we need to be. It is a divine arrangement, teaching us to respect God as the first step toward our destined path. To both women and men, remember: you do not need to compromise your values for anyone's affection. The struggle against our desires can be challenging, but patience is rewarding. If you have shown interest in someone and it's not reciprocated, just wait. Time will reveal what is meant for you.

Despite my fondness for men, I realized I had a different purpose. Discovering a purpose helps one stay committed to not engaging in casual relationships. Developing this purpose brought its own set of challenges. Enduring the pain of raising my sons without their father and suppressing my own desires was particularly tough. This was a significant struggle from my late twenties, through my thirties and forties, and now in my mid-fifties as a single mother. While some claim to be single yet engage in intimate relationships, I embraced true singleness, dedicating myself fully to my children and my purpose.

In matters of the heart, I had done years of discerning, carefully evaluating any man who caught my interest. He needed to possess specific qualities and characteristics that resonated with me. My standards were high; I was not attracted to just any man anymore. I could have pursued relationships, even dated, but I chose to dedicate my life to raising my sons. The risks of bringing a nonbiological parent into the home are well documented, with potential abuse and mistreatment. I refused to expose my sons to such dangers or to the turmoil of the wrong man entering our lives. The burden of single motherhood was already immense, and the decision to forego relationships was painful, especially in the absence of their father. A church friend once shared a harrowing story of her boyfriend tragically harming her son, which strengthened my resolve. I vowed to protect my young sons at all costs, ensuring they would never face such horrors.

In 2019, I welcomed my first grandchild, a beautiful baby girl. As I held her, all of nine pounds plus, I gazed into her eyes and felt an instant connection. When I Whispered, "You know me," she responded with a smile, and I promised her, "I won't let you down." My intention is to share my own childhood experiences with her one day, hoping it will safeguard her and guide her through life. This precious granddaughter, my first grandchild, symbolizes a new chapter. My prayer extends beyond her, to all my grandchildren, including those I may never meet, that my life lessons will provide them with strength and wisdom.

CHAPTER 12

Parents—You Are Your Child's First Role Model

My legacy is that of a single mother who raised four wonderful sons. My journey into motherhood began unexpectedly in my teens with the birth of my first son. Later, I welcomed a second son, and my family grew further with two more boys after marriage. These experiences, starting from an incredibly young age, have shaped me and underscored the profound role parents play in their children's lives. As stated before, at the immature age of nine years old, I was taken advantage of by a neighbor, by an adult, and by other chosen kin family members. Without a doubt, my sons are my greatest blessings. I would not trade them for anything in the world; they are the essence of my life, each one an integral part of my world; but I was statistically put in that 60-percent group more likely to become pregnant as a teenager.

Raising four sons single-handedly was a journey filled with challenges. Our lives were tough, and we relied on social programs like food stamps and Christmas assistance from various organizations. Food banks were our regular stops for basic needs. Housing was a struggle too, but the church stepped in, not just with material aid like clothes and shoes, but also offering spiritual guidance that was crucial in my personal growth and in providing moral support to my sons. Their moral guidance was a cornerstone in improving both my life and my children's.

Attending church became a part of our routine, like a second home where we shared meals and a sense of community with other single mothers. It was here that I met a man, related to the pastor, whom I married, leading to the addition of two more wonderful sons to our family. I am immensely proud of all of them; the older ones set an admirable example for their younger brothers.

Reflecting on these chapters of my life, I realize some stories may seem repetitive. But each retelling represents different perspectives and significant changes that shaped me, prompting deeper self-examination and personal evolution.

The Indiana Center for the Prevention of Youth Abuse & Suicide presents alarming statistics on child abuse. Before reaching eighteen, one in four girls and one in six boys experience sexual abuse. Additionally, one in five children face sexual solicitation online. A staggering 70 percent of sexual assaults reported include victims seventeen or younger, with the median age for abuse being nine. Shockingly, 85 percent of child abuse cases go unreported.

Children under twelve account for nearly half of the victims in severe cases of sexual abuse. Most disturbingly, over 90 percent of the perpetrators are individuals' children know and trust; 30 to 40 percent are family members, and 50 percent are known and trusted non-family members. Signs of abuse are not always apparent, and many children do not recognize or report their experiences as abuse.

Approximately 70 percent of child sex offenders have up to nine victims, while 20 percent have between ten and forty. An average serial child molester may have as many as four hundred victims in their lifetime. Furthermore, nearly half of the women incarcerated report having been abused as children. These statistics highlight the gravity and prevalence of child abuse. Reading them brings us closer to understanding the stark reality of this issue.

My aim is to enlighten millions of families worldwide on the importance of loving and attentively nurturing their children, going beyond just meeting their physical needs. I aspire to be an author whose books resonate with countless individuals across America and beyond, impacting lives and fostering deeper familial bonds.

Revisiting why family relationships can be complex, it is crucial to address how both men and women approach them. It is important for women to understand that their worth isn't tied to using their bodies to attract a man. A healthy relationship should be founded on mutual love and respect: a woman's respect is a form of love toward the man, and a man's love is often rooted in the respect he receives from the woman.

However, challenges arise when couples struggle with these principles. Women might believe that attracting a man with physical appearance or certain behaviors guarantees a lasting relationship, but this is often not the case. It is vital to remember that there's always someone who could potentially offer more in a relationship.

Lasting relationships are built on deeper connections beyond physical attraction or superficial qualities. Love and respect, when utterly understood and practiced, are key to nurturing a strong, enduring bond between partners.

I would like to share an insight from a male colleague of mine, who expressed that men generally appreciate natural beauty in black women. He specifically mentioned a dislike for long, artificial eyelashes. This resonated with me, as I have a similar preference; I once tried them at a local Walmart eyebrow shop and removed them within an hour. They felt inauthentic to me, as if I weren't being true to myself.

Regarding fashion, it is interesting to note that the concept of spandex pants was initially developed by a woman who intended them as a form of girdle. She adapted her stockings by cutting off the feet to create a smoother, more fitted look under her clothes. Today, these spandex pants are commonly worn in public as outerwear, which, from a certain perspective, leaves little to the imagination and can be seen as overly revealing. This change in their use reflects evolving fashion trends and societal attitudes toward modesty and self-expression.

Since my early twenties, when I reconnected with my faith, I have chosen to wear dresses and skirts every day. This change in my attire has noticeably altered how men approach me. No longer do I encounter approaches fueled by lust or disrespect. Instead, any interest shown by men tends to be more respectful and geared toward a meaningful relationship.

My experience has reinforced the idea that attire influences perception. By choosing modesty, I set a standard for how I wish to be treated—not as an object, but as a person deserving of respect. Modest dressing aligns with my spiritual beliefs and helps attract the kind of attention that aligns with my values.

There was an instance in a salon where a woman's revealing shorts led me to ponder. In a moment of reflection, I felt reaffirmed in my belief: dressing modestly in public is not just about appearance, but a statement about one's standards and choices. It is a personal decision that can have a significant impact on how one navigates relationships and is perceived by others.

I recently watched a video by Kevin Samuels on his YouTube channel, where he interviewed women of various ages from across the country. Interestingly, he often inquired about their age, dress size, and weight. These aspects, especially age and physical measurements, are significant to many women.

A notable point of discussion is the prevalence of overweight issues among many Black women, with differing opinions on attractiveness. Additionally, the use of weaves, false eyelashes, and makeup is common, which can significantly alter one's appearance. This practice sometimes obscures the natural beauty of these women, a point that is often overlooked.

For example, I had a conversation with a young colleague who usually wore long eyelashes. One day, she arrived at work without them, revealing her natural eyes. She was more beautiful in her natural state, and I made sure to tell her that. Such interactions highlight the influence of societal beauty standards on personal choices and the importance of recognizing and appreciating natural beauty.

In another segment, Kevin Samuels asked women about their financial expectations in a partner, often receiving surprisingly high figures, like $300,000. Samuels highlighted this to emphasize a disconnect; many women may not seek or realistically encounter a "high-value man," typically defined by substantial earnings. He pointed out that the average man earns around $40,000 a year, suggesting that these women's expectations were inflated.

This discussion on his channel led me to reflect on my own perspectives. As a younger woman, I never aspired to marry someone exceptionally wealthy. This might be because, despite my father fulfilling the traditional role of a provider, I was more inclined toward independence, a value often emphasized in our society.

Samuel's discussion underscores the importance of self-reflection and seeking a higher purpose. It is not just about finding a partner but understanding oneself and one's goals in life. I realized that having a purpose can be transformative. It might bring challenges and pain, but this pain is often a catalyst for growth and fulfillment. For me, my purpose was clear: to focus on raising my sons. This commitment steered me away from transient relationships and toward fulfilling my primary responsibility as a parent.

Consider the term *parents*. Embedded within it is *pair*, suggesting the involvement of two individuals. In my life, I have had to embody both roles, taking on dual jobs and managing a household that typically requires two people. This meant shouldering twice the expected responsibility. Now, as my sons have grown, I feel the physical toll of those years.

On Kevin Samuels's channel, there was a woman who left her two-year-old daughter with her eighty-year-old grandmother while she pursued a relationship. Seeking a partner is not inherently wrong, but the timing and circumstances in this case seemed inappropriate. It raises questions about prioritizing a child's well-being over personal desires.

This example reflects a broader pattern observed in some of the women who call in to the show. They appear more focused on finding a man than on more substantive life goals. It underscores the need for women to find a purpose beyond just seeking a partner—a purpose that guides and fulfills them independently.

CHAPTER 13

Women Love Men Who Remind Them of Someone as a Father Figure

As I reminisce about my childhood, I fondly remember the special moments with my father, particularly his passion for cooking. Unlike the typical cold cereal breakfasts, my father made mornings special with his extensive, hot breakfasts. His cooking was not just about feeding us; it was a way to express his love and care.

My father, originally from Pulaski, Tennessee, brought a touch of the South into our kitchen. My colleague once mentioned her visits to the South, where they savored traditional soul food. Similarly, my father delighted us with an array of delicious dishes. We had everything from fried eggs and sausage to his special hot water cornbread. The bluegill and catfish he caught himself were a family favorite, along with fried potatoes. He had a unique habit of dipping his cornbread into milk, a quirky tradition I adopted too. Oatmeal was also a staple at our breakfast table.

These culinary experiences shaped not just my palate but also my heart. They taught me the importance of nurturing and love, values I now seek in the men I meet, reminding me of the good man who raised me—my father. When I was growing up, our family dining experiences were far from lavish or fast-food oriented. My father, a man of simple tastes, never brought us McDonald's or indulged in the typical fast-food outings. Similarly, the excitement of pizza deliveries was something we never experienced. Our household staples were humble yet nourishing—potatoes, beans, and sugar were the mainstays in our pantry.

Our meals, often repetitive, consisted of these simple ingredients. Once the cooked food was consumed, we were left with these basic items until the next grocery trip. As children, we learned early on not to be meticulous eaters. The luxury of choice was not part of our culinary vocabulary. We ate what was served, appreciating the sustenance it provided. This upbringing instilled in us a sense of gratitude and an understanding of the value of simplicity.

Despite his struggles with alcohol, my father had a unique way of caring for our family. He was often referred to as a "responsible alcoholic" because of his ability to balance his personal challenges with family responsibilities. He shared his love for the outdoors with us, taking us along on fishing and hunting trips with my older brothers and their friends. I vividly remember a meal of barbecued rabbit, a dish we never had again.

My father was resourceful, especially in the face of wasteful practices by local food stores. He was troubled by their habit of discarding decent food, such as greens like mustard, collard, kale, or turnip—not lettuce—which he would rescue from dumpsters. He had a talent for cooking these greens in such a way that they tasted as rich and flavorful as meat.

He also had a special skill in making corn wine, a recipe that unfortunately passed away with him. It was the best-tasting wine, unique in that it was not intoxicating. We even tasted it occasionally under his supervision.

There is a story he once shared about finding a whole ham discarded by a store. He retrieved it and cooked it to perfection. The origins of our meals were often a mystery, but one thing was clear—we never fell ill from anything he prepared. His ingenuity in the kitchen provided us in ways that were both unconventional and nurturing.

Reflecting on my childhood as an older woman now, I recognize the persistent scarcity of food we faced at home. My actions were not driven by a desire for trouble or danger; rather, they were influenced by a basic need. I often found myself gravitating towards friends whose homes were assured of regular, hearty meals. Their parents would serve dinner, providing a sense of normalcy and fulfillment that was lacking in my own home sometimes.

My father, aware of our situation, would frequently take us to visit relatives. These visits were more than just familial obligations; they were a subtle strategy to ensure we had enough to eat. In our own home, dinners were simple yet satisfying. My sister would often cook fried pork steaks and spaghetti, usually without meat. Despite the simplicity, these meals were always delicious and cooked with care.

Visits to my aunties' homes were a different culinary experience. They were all enthusiastic cooks, ensuring there was always something to eat. Often, they would prepare meals in anticipation of our arrival. Beyond the nourishment they provided, these visits were filled with family conversations and laughter, making each meal about more than just food—they were gatherings of love and care. My father had an entrepreneurial spirit, evident in his side hustles. He crafted grills from steel barrels, a skill that was both creative and practical. Additionally, he collected recyclable materials like aluminum cans, copper, and newspapers, which he then sold to the local scrapyard for extra income. This resourcefulness not only contributed to our family's finances but also set a strong example for me.

I have come to realize that women often appreciate men who remind them of positive male figures from their lives, men like my father, who hustled tirelessly for his family. He always ensured we had transportation, maintaining a truck and a car to support his various ventures. My brother and I have fond memories of riding in the back of his truck on numerous occasions.

In our family, and even extending to our cousins, there was a belief that a man should have his own transportation, symbolizing responsibility, and stability. My father also had a pragmatic view on food; he believed that cooking in hot grease could "kill anything," leading him to buy fried chicken and fish from specific restaurants known for these dishes.

Additionally, my father had invested in quality fishing gear over time, an investment that would be quite valuable today. The money he earned from his odd jobs, including making those steel grills, partly went into acquiring this gear. Interestingly, one of his grills' designs has left a legacy. In Indiana, a popular restaurant named King Ribs, with two to three locations, uses the same large steel grills to barbecue their meat. A testament to my father's craftsmanship and enduring influence, even though my father had nothing to do with creating those grills. He sold many of his own by his handiwork.

At twelve or thirteen years old, I used to visit an elderly man in the neighborhood, following in the footsteps of a friend who also visited him. He often talked about Art Linkletter, a name I did not recognize, but I sat and listened, viewing him as a sort of father figure in my youthful innocence. I had no romantic relationships or children at that age; my visits were purely for companionship and guidance.

The old man often spoke about life and the influence of friends, advising me not to simply follow them nor be like them. Although I heard his words, I did not truly absorb them. My main attraction to these visits was the treats he gave—cookies, cakes, and sweets—the same treats he gave to my friend. I remember hesitantly asking him for sweets, and sometimes even for money.

Reflecting on it now, I recognize the naivety and potential danger in my actions. If it had been my daughter, I would have advised her against such behavior. There is a lesson in understanding that asking favors can sometimes lead to uncomfortable or unexpected situations. This lesson hit home one day when I decided to clean his cluttered kitchen, thinking I was doing something helpful. But when he acted inappropriately toward me, it was a stark and painful realization of the risks involved. That incident marked the end of my visits for treats and money, a jarring experience that highlighted the vulnerabilities of a young girl in such a situation.

In my growing up years, our neighborhood was blessed with an abundance of fruit trees that seemed like nature's gift to us children. We had apple trees in a nearby open field, and just across our alley, a neighbor's fenced backyard boasted two more apple trees. Our own yard was graced with a pear tree, and another yard in the neighborhood had a grapevine. But my absolute favorite was a yard with a cherry tree, which seemed to be made just for our delight.

We would spend hours climbing these trees, plucking the fruits directly and eating them right there, without even thinking of taking them home to wash. I remember my mouth itching from the unwashed fruits, but miraculously, I never fell ill. Often, I would wander down the alley without any reason, only to find my friends playing outside. To us as children, it did not matter whether we were in the alley or the street; the joy was simply in being outside, playing and enjoying the natural bounty of our neighborhood.

One day, to enjoy some candy by myself, I walked through the alley to make my purchase. Unfortunately, this decision led to an upsetting incident. Several of my young friends noticed the candy and reacted harshly. They took turns hitting me, which left me in tears. It was a painful experience, not just physically but emotionally, as these were children, I considered friends.

The situation was further compounded by the one who was violating me from the neighborhood, someone who had been harming me at his house but at the street corner house of some more friends who lived there. He orchestrated a more distressing situation by involving other boys, who were cousins of my friends. Under his watch, they physically overpowered me, although I remained clothed. This experience was deeply traumatic, marking a significant and painful chapter in my childhood, filled with betrayal and vulnerability.

CHAPTER 14

Barefoot Memories: Navigating Childhood Adversity and the Quest for Belonging

Growing up, I was often in the company of four sisters who had a large extended family in the neighborhood. It felt like they had an abundance of relatives, while I felt isolated and many times alone. My own siblings were much older and occupied with their own lives. The sisters, whom I spent a lot of time with, were regularly dropped off by their mother at a street corner. They had to remove their shoes and walk barefoot. Despite this, their mother always ensured they were neatly dressed and their hair well-groomed. Similarly, I often walked barefoot, occasionally injuring my toe but continuing to play. This highlights the importance of supervising children. Due to lack of foot care knowledge and resources, my feet have suffered long-term effects. We were a poor family, with my mother frequently walking or using city buses, neglecting her own foot care, and often removing calluses. Foot care was not a priority for us then, but I have since realized its importance, especially after undergoing a foot operation in my later years.

In my childhood neighborhood, we creatively played without conventional toys. One of our favorite activities involved old tires; we would climb inside them and have someone push us down a hill for a thrilling ride. I owned a bicycle, but it had seen better days due to my brother's fondness for performing wheelies, leaving it damaged beyond my ability to repair. This bike, often referred to as a "bus bike," was in such a state that it had no tires. I remember riding it down the streets on just its frames. A vivid memory from those days is the ice cream truck, Mr. Frosty. The familiar jingle of the truck would send me running home to ask my mother for some money to buy a treat.

As a child, around ten or eleven years old, I cooked in a modest kitchen. I was peeling potatoes and frying them in a pan on a gas stove. The kitchen has a simple table against the wall with one chair, where my father always sat. The scene also includes an old washing machine with a wringer in our unmodernized basement. There is a clothesline over the stove with some clothes hanging from it. The kitchen window allows a view of another clothesline outside, with more clothes pinned to it. The overall atmosphere is one of a humble household, with a focus on the child's independence and resourcefulness in cooking. My parents somehow knew that I would not burn the house down, and handwashing my own clothes was not a problem. I grew up rough, and the lessons learned were that I took those difficult complexities of life challenges, and they helped me shape my life even while raising my sons.

Reflecting on my school days, I remember excelling academically, yet I faced a significant challenge: a lack of clothing. With my parents managing limited resources for our family of six, we had to make do with extraordinarily little. This situation made me a target at school, where I endured bullying and was often coerced into physical confrontations, a common one being the provocation of the first one knocking a stick the shoulder. Resisting these fights was not an option, as it would only lead to further aggression.

I disliked fighting, aware of the potential harm it could bring. A vivid memory that stands out is the day I decided to take utensil out the kitchen, intending to defend myself in a fight that already had started in my neighborhood with a friend. We later became best friends. She was the one who grabbed my arm, saving my life at a neighborhood party that escalated to violence. However, as I was about to leave the house, my mother intervened, taking the utensil from my hand. Looking back, I am immensely grateful for her action, recognizing how it prevented a disastrous outcome. This experience remains a poignant reminder of the struggles I faced and the importance of my mother's protective presence in my life.

We engaged in various games like kickball, curve ball, football, karate, jump rope, hopscotch, Monopoly, Uno, cards, checkers, and jacks, but I did not own any of these, not even the balls. During football games, when my girlfriends and I joined the boys and their cousins, two boys would often hit us in the eyes if we made mistakes. I kept silent about this abuse due to fear and the ingrained belief that reporting it was wrong. This experience, along with other past incidents, has left me with persistent dark circles around my eyes. I am not sure if they are a direct result from those childhood events, but they have been a part of me for years. Once, after getting my eyebrows shaped, an employee complimented my "eyeshadow," not realizing that the darkness was a result of my past, not makeup.

My brother and I often engaged in daring activities, like chasing the bus after it passed our house. To wake us up for school, my mother would pour tiny amounts of water on our faces. We did not have a fixed bedtime. A vivid memory from second grade involves an incident in Mrs. Haskins's class. Desperately needing the restroom, I raised my hand, but before I could leave, I had an accident in my sailor dress right at my desk. This event marked the beginning of a difficult period at school; I was constantly ridiculed and falsely labeled as unclean, even while enduring molestation and physical punishment from a neighbor. In sixth grade, my classmates cruelly wrote on their hands, "Get your Molly shot," a taunt that persisted until junior high. To cope, I often pretended to catch the bus, only to hide in my parents' house all day in the basement, reemerging only when the buses returned. Despite these challenges, my teachers, including Mr. Lane in high school mathematics, always praised my cursive writing.

Despite performing well academically, I was often embarrassed about attending school due to a lack of adequate clothing and shoes. As I grew older, I cared less about fashion, unlike many women. However, I also faced challenges with obesity from my mid-thirties onwards. A vivid memory from my youth is of a time when my girlfriend and I took the city bus downtown to shoplift clothes. Unfortunately, we were caught. My mother, who had always been proud of my law-abiding nature, was so shocked that she hired an attorney for me. This experience taught me the importance of careful parenting, as I had previously heard about stealing and was curious to try it. The incident ended with us being escorted by a police officer back into the store and then to the juvenile detention center in a paddy wagon, even as my friend casually ate the candy given to her by the police officers on duty even though she had also stolen. I spent two weekends in juvenile detention, walking there on my own initiative, deeply embarrassed by the thought of our neighbors finding out. During this time, I was unnecessarily sprayed for lice, despite not having any.

In high school, I was initially bussed to a township school, which I really enjoyed. There, we had facilities to take showers and style our hair with hot combs. However, my mother was concerned about the distance and arranged a transfer to a local high school. I liked this school too, especially as it had a more diverse student body with a higher proportion of Black students. Reflecting on my junior high school years, I am amazed I passed my classes, given my frequent absences. Socially, it was challenging; many girls did not like me. On the last day of school, I was warned that I was a target for a physical attack, which made me yearn to just stay home.

During my childhood, there was a local store called Cash Bargain Center known for selling reject clothing. Around corner was a Burger Chef, a fast-food restaurant beckoned often my friends and I made an inviting continual feast to eat the pickles off the buffet-style table advertised to build a hearty sandwich with many other inviting vegetables we ignored; I don't know who had the funds to buy, but it was an inviting accomplish what we came for. Back to the local reject clothing store: these clothes often had noticeable stitching, and the store's perfume cost less than a dollar. Once, my mother excitedly bought my brother and I sneakers in a mix of orange, red, and blue. However, wearing this attracted mockery from other children, who sang a teasing song: "Buddies, they make your feet feel funny; Buddies, they cost a $1.99." Another time, my mother brought home a pair of "Tracks" tennis shoes, which I absolutely adored, as they were fashionable. She also gave me bellbottom jeans adorned with rhinestones and designs. Unfortunately, bellbottoms were not in vogue then; straight-leg jeans were the trend, so I never wore them.

All my siblings, save for one, are alive, and each pursued their own endeavors. My sister worked at St. Francis de Sales Nursery, while my brother collected pop bottles and ran a newspaper route. My oldest brother embarked on a career with USP, another brother joined the Marines, and one faced life with disabilities. My sister's life took a sharp turn when she became pregnant at fourteen and married young. This meant less time with her, though I frequently visited her new home, three miles away. I recall trying to shield her from her husband, who seemed like a stranger intruding on our bond. My sister, once a constant in my life, combing and straightening my hair, and responsible for bringing my beloved baby doll each Christmas, was now married and living elsewhere. Although I had other siblings nearby, their involvement in my life was limited, leaving me longing for the care and attention once abundantly shared.

My older brothers had active social lives, dating girlfriends, and occasionally indulging in smoking and drinking TJ Swan. One brother would enlist my help for odd tasks like picking his toes and practicing dance moves for parties. He eventually married a schoolteacher who later became a principal. She was wonderful to me, taking me clothes shopping and introducing me to makeup, which I grew to love until she asked my brother to tell me to stop using hers.

Witnessing this brother move from the ghetto to the suburbs and improve his life was inspiring. However, during this period, I became involved with my sons' father and got pregnant. The clothes my sister-in-law bought me no longer fit, and on my sixteenth birthday, I made the tough decision to quit school, as it was not common to see pregnant girls there. By eighteen, I was a mother of two sons.

I vividly recall the day I discovered I was pregnant, sitting on my parents' back porch, gazing skyward, uttering in despair to God, "You can't even help me." It was in this moment of surrender that God responded to my plea. My older brother pulled up in his station wagon around that time. I was about four months along. He casually asked if I fancied a ride. Had he mentioned church, I might have declined, but a ride seemed appealing. Consequently, I ended up staying long enough to be invited to a church service. Spending that night there marked the beginning of a profound change in my life. It felt like stepping out of darkness into light.

Seeking wisdom is essential, and it's a journey often influenced by our upbringing and experiences. Many of us learn through the assumption that we will eventually figure things out on our own. Parents play a crucial role in guiding and educating their children, but sometimes they might not be aware of the challenges their children are facing. The phrase "experience is the best teacher" can be true, yet it is not always the easiest or the safest way to learn. Growing up, I found it difficult to confide in others, even in safe spaces like church. This hesitance to speak can carry into adulthood, leading to a preference for solitude and a reluctance to voice concerns. It is also challenging as a child to discern whom to trust and befriend. In my case, even in the shared space of a church, I attended with my abuser's family, I had to make tough choices about where to seek refuge and support. The courage to speak up and make these decisions often comes later in life, not during childhood.

CHAPTER 15

Struggling, Striving, and Thriving: Journey of Resilience as a Wife, Mother, and Family Toward Independence

Growing up, I yearned for adulthood, believing it would empower me to defend myself. As a child, around nine years old, I often found solace in the solitude of my parents' porch, tearfully feeling unloved and isolated. My upbringing emphasized self-reliance. My father's words, "Go to school to learn the rules so you don't be no fool," echoed in my mind, but they felt insufficient for the challenges I faced. I was determined not to be the outlier in my family, and so, at nineteen, I graduated from high school, balancing the responsibilities of being a mother to two children with my studies at Beauty College. However, my path took a turn when I agreed to my husband's request for a leave of absence from the cosmetology college, a return to which became impossible when the institution, along with other beauty colleges, went bankrupt. This twist in my journey led us to establish a family business, an idea primarily driven by my husband but supported by all of us. For a while, it seemed like a brilliant solution.

Reflecting on how society educates women, it is clear that there's a strong emphasis on gaining education, achieving independence, and acquiring personal assets without relying on a male partner. This message, "You don't need a man," becomes deeply embedded, particularly for those who have faced childhood traumas or challenging relationships. Imagine the life of a young mother, managing parenthood alone, facing financial difficulties, and feeling isolated and unable to speak out against injustices. Such experiences can lead to long-term issues with self-esteem and self-care, often overlooked in the societal narrative about women's resilience.

This is not a call for sympathy, but rather a reminder of the importance of attentive parenting. Children of all ages need our undivided attention and understanding. It is crucial to educate young girls about personal boundaries and the importance of consent. Additionally, the idea of teaching celibacy as a lifestyle choice is worth considering, especially when looking at cultures where arranged marriages are common and divorce rates are notably low. This perspective urges a re-evaluation of the lessons we impart to children, ensuring they grow up with a balanced understanding of independence, relationships, and self-worth.

I have been blessed with four wonderful sons, each bringing unique joy into my life. A neighbor of mine, who has three sons, once mentioned that God's intention was for her to feel loved. I resonate with that sentiment, believing that God intended for me to be cherished as well. There's a natural balance in relationships: men loving women, and women respecting men. Reflecting on my sons, I see how they have been my protectors. One of my sons, when he was around ten, would tenderly care for my feet, massaging them and applying lotion. My eldest son, interestingly, harbored the notion that married couples do not have children, showing his protective instinct over me. I recall an incident in a store with one of my younger sons. We encountered a colleague of mine, someone I had a liking for, though it never developed into anything. My son, sensing my feelings, commented, "I hope we don't see him often," showcasing his protective nature even at a young tender age.

Reflecting on the man I admired but never truly got to know, I remember how he was employed at a place I had long aspired to work at, long before our paths crossed. My interest in that workplace began during my marriage, driven by a desire for a higher-paying job. The concept of some people being "bridges" in our lives did not resonate with me until I heard one of my sons mention it, a phrase he learned from a friend. At the time, I was working at a hospital, earning just slightly above minimum wage. As a single, divorced mother with four children, this job was crucial, yet barely sufficient. I had a brief stint at his workplace as a Christmas helper, where, astonishingly, I earned more in four to five hours than I did in my regular seven-hour job with benefits. This experience prompted me to apply for a position at his company, knowing the financial stability and benefits it could offer.

This is my story. I did not have a car, and there was a job opening hiring for the Post Office of all positions at a local hotel just up the street from my workplace. I had tried to secure a position there before but always failed the required test. Fortunately, the hotel was offering classes to help applicants pass this test. Eager for this opportunity, I enrolled and began commuting by bus to the downtown location where the classes were held. Originally scheduled for three weeks, the classes extended to six weeks, and I decided to attend the full duration on a payment schedule to take the classes. My dedication paid off; I excelled in the class and later achieved high scores on the job's test, which was divided into two parts. A year later, I was offered the job. This role was crucial for me, especially in supporting my sons financially. It came at a pivotal time, as the hospital where I worked was downsizing. Thankfully, I had already moved on by then.

Do you recall when I mentioned that you might not end up with the person you desire, but God will ensure you gain what you need and some of what you want from that relationship, especially when there is no sin or harm involved? There is always something to be gained. God, who sees into our souls, knows everything. God embodies love. Shouldn't a man understand that a good partner is what a woman needs? I once heard in a movie that a woman's love for a man is precious and should not be dismissed. To him, she offers her best. Such love should not be suppressed. I've experienced deep love for a man myself, and I know once that love fades, he loses a part of me. If that love was genuine, we no longer yearn for that man. But when we genuinely love, we are willing to do everything to bring joy into the relationship and make it work and to please that man.

Navigating single motherhood since my late twenties, through my thirties and forties, and now in my mid-fifties, has brought its share of challenges. Over time, I developed some resentment. It is easy for a woman in my situation to grow tough, to become complacent, which isn't ideal. While I was content, I knew I could aspire to be more, to do more—as I am striving to do now through authoring this book, hoping to help others. I have been inspired by Steve Harvey's advice on a YouTube channel, with the desire to pen down a list of three hundred desires. Surprisingly, one of these was to find a partner, specifically my ninety-fifth wish. Requesting this from God made me feel uneasy. Again, this book is not a prerequisite for a partner, but merely a profound focus on seeing children getting shaped to become productive souls for our society.

CHAPTER 16

Growth and Dreams– A Single Mom's Journey

For a while, I mistook my complacency for contentment. I told myself that accepting life as it comes was enough. But I have learned there's a fine line between the two. Complacency is losing yourself, while true contentment is finding joy and satisfaction within.

As a single mom, I have faced the loss of my children's fathers. I had resigned myself to a life alone, convinced that this was my unchangeable fate. However, I have come to realize that life is not just about accepting what is given but also about seeking what can be.

The scripture from 1 Timothy 6:6-8 resonates deeply with me: "But godliness with contentment is great gain. For we brought nothing into this world, and it is certain we can carry nothing out. And having food and raiment, let us be therewith content." These words remind me that while our material journey is transient, our spiritual and emotional growth is perpetual.

I have learned that as a single mother, there's always room to grow. My dreams do not have to be secondary to my circumstances. By embracing both the challenges and the joys of my journey, I am rediscovering my purpose and rekindling.

There are moments in life when it feels like the universe is sending us a message, a nudge to wake us up to new possibilities. I experienced one such moment, quite unexpectedly, on a regular Saturday morning.

As I was browsing through YouTube, a random thought crossed my mind: "What if I lost the weight?" At that time, my interest in romantic relationships was nonexistent; neither men nor women caught my fancy. My struggle with obesity was real, yet I was young and, in my own way, content. Or so I believed.

Then, a video popped up on my screen. It featured a man giving a tour of his house. This happened while I was sitting in my car, trying to find a parking spot at a local grocery store, with Anita Baker's soulful voice playing in the background. It struck me as odd—why would someone broadcast their home like that? It is not like he was selling it.

But in that moment, watching this man's simple act of sharing his space, something clicked inside me. It made me realize how God truly knows us better than we know ourselves. This trivial video was, in fact, a profound moment of clarity for me. This was a pivotal moment in my life as a thought came to me: "I'm going to change my life." I was inspired to see this person walking while doing something I would one hope to do one day. I have dreamed of living in a warmer state where I could regularly have visits from family and friends in enjoying unforgettable moments.

In my quest to discover the best places to live in Florida, I stumbled upon a YouTube channel that showcased a stunning house. The owner resided in the southern state where I had longed to live. This encounter recalled a conversation I had with my father in our kitchen years ago. I was about twelve or thirteen then, without any children of my own. He had told me that to find a good man, I might have to look toward the South.

Was this the man my father spoke of? It is hard to say. The South is vast, home to many men, and I am not advertising myself as an offer of a date. At times in our lives, God works in mysterious ways to get our attention, to get to a place where he wants us to be to reach our purpose. Yet this man captivated my attention in an unexpected way. His channel was not about finding love or relationships; it was focused on finances, wealth-building, passive income, credit scores, stocks, and assets. He spoke about a topic often shied away from—money. His insights and wisdom left me deeply impressed.

It dawned on me then how God works in mysterious ways to draw our attention toward our true calling, our divine purpose. This chance encounter was more than about finding a beautiful place to live or learning about finances. It was a nudge from the universe, guiding me to become the woman God intended me to be."

I believe it is important for young people to learn early about the responsibilities of being a spouse. Observing my children has been enlightening. My two eldest sons, without my guidance, understood the traditional approach to relationships. They knew to seek a young lady's father's permission first. My second son, currently the only one married, followed this practice. He asked for his now-wife's hand in marriage, which was challenging due to differing religious beliefs. He embraced her faith, and they now share a strong marriage and with my wonderful grandson. My eldest son, still young and not ready for marriage, respectfully approached a young lady's father for permission to take his daughter to lunch. The father declined, but as a mother, I admired his respectfulness in not pursuing her without her father's approval.

I have a granddaughter. I have made it a point to educate her about personal safety from an early age. I have taught her that no one should touch her private areas and that if anyone ever does, she should tell a trusted adult like her grandmother, mother, father, or her maternal grandmothers. I have also instructed her not to talk to strangers. It is crucial to supervise young children during outdoor play and not let them go outside alone. As children grow, it is important to teach them to ask permission before doing things, helping them understand they don't have an inherent right to everything. This is crucial for their safety and sense of responsibility. My own childhood experience, where a lack of awareness led to a traumatic incident, has taught me never to underestimate the importance of vigilance, regardless of how safe a neighborhood may appear. Whether in the suburbs or a well-maintained older area, the safety of children should never be taken for granted.

CHAPTER 17

Believe It or Not—Parental Guidance as an Expression of Love

As a child, I never imagined that a simple act of playing outside our home and walking in what was believed to be a safe neighborhood could lead to such a traumatic experience. At nine years old, during these innocent adventures, I faced an unthinkable incident involving the oldest brother of a close friend. This harrowing experience left me distraught, often finding myself in tears on my mother's porch, overwhelmed by a sense of being unloved.

In our family's backyard, we had two German shepherds, Butch and Bullet, both perpetually chained. My father passionately but firmly believed that dogs belonged outside, not in the house. Consequently, Butch, positioned closer to the house, was the only one provided with a doghouse.

Our interactions with them were minimal. Neither playtime nor affectionate gestures were common; it was usually my parents who took on the task of feeding them. Tragically, Bullet once attempted to leap over the fence but, in a heart-wrenching accident, ended up hanging himself and did not survive. Butch, more isolated near his doghouse, remained the sole canine presence in our backyard after Bullet's demise.

When I was about eight or nine years old, I had a harrowing encounter with Butch. One day, feeling brave, I approached him as he sat quietly on the ground. Without any warning or a growl, Butch attacked me the moment I gently rubbed his back. I found myself running toward the house in tears, blood trailing behind me. The severity of the situation led to an ambulance being called, and I was rushed to the hospital.

In the aftermath, the dog pound took Butch away. However, the response from my family was not what one might expect. There were no comforting words, no expressions of relief or love, no hugs. Instead, I faced a barrage of questions that seemed to blame me for the incident. Queries like "Did he bite you or scratch you?" dominated the conversation, overshadowing any concern for my well-being. This response felt even more isolating as I was the darkest-skinned member of my family, a detail that, in my mind, was inescapably linked to their reaction."

Despite the challenges, I have come to forgive and love my family unconditionally. After the incident with Butch, my mother's small act of giving me popsicles while my face was healing brought me comfort, especially since I could not eat solid food. Interestingly, over the years, many have mistaken my scar for a dimple. It is as if through some divine intervention, the scar was transformed, giving the appearance of a natural dimple.

This feature has interestingly echoed through my family. A few of my sons were born with dimples, and even my granddaughter shares this trait. It is a fascinating genetic twist!

My mother often worried about how the scar might affect my relationships. She wondered if boys would be deterred by it or if I could ever see past it myself. These concerns led me to contemplate plastic surgery on numerous occasions. But the journey of accepting my scar has been an integral part of my story.

When I was around fifteen years old and pregnant, I faced the discomfort of morning sickness. One day, as I was walking home from my sister and brother-in-law's apartment, a trek I often made, covering about three miles, I found myself needing to pass through a large park. This park, familiar from my childhood, was where we used to enjoy free concerts and box lunches. It also held fond memories of the Indianapolis Zoo, which was once a part of it.

On this day, I stopped to rest on a park bench. There, I casually noticed a man fiddling with his bicycle. Not paying much attention, I soon stood up and began to walk down a hill in the park. Unexpectedly and shockingly, this man jogged past me in a state of nudity and made a disturbing request. Alarmed and frightened, I ran as fast as I could, not stopping until I reached the safety of my home.

In my childhood, if I wanted to see a friend, I would usually walk over. My mother often had to search for me, as we lacked effective communication means. We did not own a phone for a long time, and when we did, it wasn't for long, due to affordability issues. Without strong parental guidance, I felt free to do as I pleased. Sometimes, I wished my parents were more assertive, saying, "No, you can't do that," or "You have chores," or even "Stay home." Contrary to what some might think, children desire guidance. They feel vulnerable and seek direction, even if they cannot articulate it.

There were instances where men whistled at us as we walked down the street. One evening, while heading to an acquaintance's apartment, a car pulled over. Two of my friends approached it and ended up getting in, leaving another friend and me behind. I felt it was unsafe, so we didn't join them. Instead, we returned to my friend's apartment and informed her mother about the situation. Surprisingly, she did not react much; she didn't contact the police or report them missing. When my friends returned, they had been left on the opposite side of town by those men. Rumors circulated about some sexual encounters that might have happened during that time.

I recall a time when I was fourteen and had a boyfriend who was seventeen. He worked at a fast-food restaurant and owned a car. One day, he took me to his house to introduce me to his mother. Reflecting on it now as I author this book, I realize he must have had genuine feelings for me. Meeting someone's mother is a significant step. Later, he joined the military, built a career there, and I heard he married a woman from another country. Back then, it seemed like everyone had a boyfriend, or was about to have one soon.

I remember meeting their grandfather, and his wife, my two oldest sons' grandparents on their fathers' side. I was thrilled during my visit to their house. It was an impeccably maintained, spacious old colonial home, complete with multiple bedrooms, an upstairs, and a basement. It was evident that my sons' father had been raised well. At that time, I was seen as an eighteen-year-old because my friend had misled him about my age, an act of deceit I never corrected. I was just eager to be around friends. I recall his stepmother cooking chili that day, stirring a pot with noticeably few noodles in it, just like the way I prepare my chili now, with just a few strands of spaghetti. He mentioned his father had advised him to stay away from me. Eventually, he discovered my real age, but by then, it was too late. I had hoped he would marry me when I was sixteen, but when I brought it up, he simply echoed my question, "You want to get married?"

He was seldom present for prolonged periods, though he occasionally appeared, like during Christmas. Surprisingly, when I was about twenty-three, he proposed marriage unexpectedly. I declined but shared his proposal with a church member. Nothing further developed between us, and I regret not facilitating more time for him to be with his sons. I have learned that as a single mother, it's important not to let others prevent the father from seeing his children or you, provided he or she isn't troublesome. The relationship extends beyond just you; it is about the child too.

I would not trade my sons for anything, even if I was offered payment. We grew up together, often rushing to catch city buses. Although the rides were lengthy from one place to another, we enjoyed ourselves and adapted to it. Once, in a heavy downpour, I was offered a ride while waiting on a street corner under a heavy downpour from a stranger to get to work. My straightforwardness about not having my own transport moved her to tears. I was determined to provide for my children, even if it meant spending the entire day on buses. My mother, too, was unfazed by public transport; she never depended on anyone else. She would go wherever she needed within the city. I admire her for that resilience, a trait I embraced myself after leaving home at twenty years old.

The phrase "tied to the hip" perfectly describes my relationship with my sons. I took them everywhere I went, except to work. I worked as a cook in schools and, during the summer, served free lunches in summer programs. Reflecting on the marriage proposal from my sons' father, I chose to wait for the father of my two younger sons. However, my marriage did not turn out as I had hoped. I had envisioned a lifelong union. Looking back, I wish I had taken more time to consider my decisions. This highlights the importance of parental guidance. Though they might not have known, I believe someone did. I needed someone to talk to during those times.

CHAPTER 18

Understanding the Significance of Purpose in Life

My journey has been challenging, marked by unwelcome and inappropriate situations that I should have avoided or spoken up against, including in my marriage. My advice is to vigilantly watch over your children. I am thankful for having survived and reached this point in my life, recognizing that certain people were brought into and removed from my life for my betterment. I hope this book benefits many families, or even just one—whether it is a family, an adult, a woman, a man, or a pair of parents. My aim is for my experiences to safeguard children, ensuring they can enjoy a carefree childhood, feeling loved and protected by their parents or a trusted guardian. It is crucial not to assume that neighborhoods, relatives, communities, or friends are inherently safe. This book is not meant to instill fear about your children's safety. Rather, it is a call to action: watch them, talk to them, love, listen, play with, guide, instruct, discipline, read to, feed, and clothe them. Remember, they are precious.

Did you know that the act of giving of intimacy signifies a profound giving of oneself? When a woman engages intimately with a man, she shares a deep part of herself. She has given this man everything, and she thinks that part is just a part of the relationship. You hear of a woman finds it hard to give up a man even if she is being mistreated that is the reason she stays with him. It is a sense of belonging, a type of marriage that wasn't under an oath of two to three witnesses. This is true for anyone, regardless of their achievements or possessions, like a career, wealth, or fame. Reflect on the traditional phrase, "he gave her away." It symbolizes a father entrusting his daughter to another man in marriage. It is crucial to understand that intimacy is ideally a mature act, meant for a marital bond. A child, not ready for such experiences, loses a sense of innocence and guidance from parents when exposed prematurely to adult intimacy. This is akin to forcing a child to drive a car—overwhelming and inappropriate. Children primarily need love, guidance, and care from their parents. In a wedding, we celebrate "holy matrimony," signifying a union that transcends mere physicality, reminding us of the deeper commitments and responsibilities involved.

You might question, given my awareness, how I could lead a promiscuous life. This phase spanned from ages eighteen to twenty, concluding when I joined a local church and later married at twenty-five. Though initially planned to marry at twenty-one, I chose to wait. As a single woman, I raised my first two sons alone, embracing a celibate lifestyle and attending church regularly, believing in eventual marriage. It was through the church that I met people who influenced my transformation into a better mother. They offered truth and guidance. I felt a strong urge to improve as a mother; failing to do so seemed like it would lead to a dire outcome, as if my very survival depended on it.

I reached out to my church's pastor for counseling. Adversity often reveals one's true character. Post-divorce, at twenty-nine, turning thirty, I made a firm decision to raise my four sons alone in our two-bedroom apartment, without reverting to a promiscuous lifestyle. I resolved that my sons would not call another man "Daddy" unless their biological fathers chose to be part of their lives. I believe those fathers should have fought to be involved. Even if it meant challenging me, they needed to show determination and persistence for their sons. Sadly, one father ceased to be involved, and the other, whom I had married and divorced, threatened that if he got custody, I would never see them again. This alarming statement was shared with my divorce attorney. He had a substance abuse issue and would need to navigate the legal system to regain visitation rights.

Reflecting on my past, one of my sons remarked, "Mom, all I remember is you constantly working." Now, he is an adult, married with a wonderful wife and son. I prioritized my sons' well-being, striving to protect them and fulfill my role as a mother while juggling two jobs, until I could secure a single, better-paying position. In marriage, as in any partnership, failing to plan is planning to fail. It is crucial to bring as much as possible to the table for open discussion, ensuring a foundation for mutual understanding and support.

My initial job was at McDonald's, where I earned $3.35 an hour. I was eighteen, already a mother to two young children. The opportunity came through my sister-in-law's cousin, who worked there as a manager and helped me get the job. This support was crucial, enabling me to afford an apartment and live independently with my sons. I am deeply grateful for that assistance. This job marked the start of my journey toward self-reliance, teaching me not to fear employment. My father always advised, "Be the best in your work, even if it's mopping floors." His words resonated with me, and I was honored with the award for "Best Lobby Person" during my tenure there—an accolade I proudly keep to this day. I worked at McDonald's for a year.

My next role was as a cook in various public-school cafeterias, serving school-aged children, until I secured a permanent position at one school. The hiring manager appointed me as the head cook, a manager, even though I was just twenty-one and overseeing women old enough to be my mother, many of whom were grandmothers. Our task was to prepare meals for five hundred to six hundred children, plus teachers and administrators, with the head cook responsible for the main course. A colleague and friend, an older woman named Florida, whom we affectionately called Flo, was instrumental in training me to cook for the entire school. Initially, I mistook her rigorous training for bullying because of my age. After I discussed my concerns with my pastor, he suggested she was helping me. However, it later emerged that Flo desired my position. Eventually, I was demoted, and Flo took over. She had assumed the role came with a high salary, but in reality, I was earning barely more than four dollars an hour. A subsequent disagreement between Flo and our supervisor led to her being replaced, and the position was handed back to me.

My daily routine involved extensive bus travel. I first took a bus to drop my sons off at my parents for babysitting, then caught another bus to work. After work, I rode the city bus back to my parents' walking a block to and from their house.

Then, I would take the bus again, heading home across town. This involved transferring buses downtown, with the second bus bringing us home. This commute was a five-day-a-week affair, only altered if schools closed due to weather.

Reflecting on my friend Florida, affectionately known as Flo, her name had an interesting backstory. Her mother named her after the state of Florida, a place she adored. Despite this, I initially had little interest in visiting Florida myself. However, when my sister invited me on a trip there, I accepted, and to my surprise, had an incredible time, especially with family. Remarkably, I was forty-nine at the time and had never taken a vacation before. I used to think vacations were a luxury only for those without financial worries, not for someone like me. Florida, famous for its appeal to tourists, Walt Disney World, and resorts, inspired me to invite others, including a neighbor, to join. We visited three parks in Walt Disney World and stayed at a resort. The experience was thrilling, except for my fear of flying. That required some prayer and fasting to overcome.

When my son invited me to San Diego, I was overwhelmed with fear, even breaking down in tears, saying I could not go. However, he was persistent. My only previous flying experience had been to Texas with my first two sons, and back then, I had not thought much about it until boarding the plane. To calm my nerves, I met the pilot and was shown the control panel in the cockpit. Though I did not understand what I was seeing, learning there were three people in the cockpit was somewhat reassuring.

I visited Florida at least two other times, driving there with one of my sons. On my second visit, I noticed a change in how I felt about the state. It stirred a desire in me to live there. During my first visit, we did not see any beaches, but the second time was different. Seeing palm trees and the ocean for the first time was astounding.

When I was growing up, my only view of the ocean was through television, and I used to draw Mickey Mouse, because it was easy and recognizable. The sight of tall palm trees was exhilarating, and at forty-nine, I even hugged one. These experiences were a gift from Florida Morris, my friend who passed away. It felt like her way of ensuring I would always remember her. One of my elder sons once made his home in the bustling city of Morris. He carved out a successful life for himself, securing a rewarding career and settling into a comfortable apartment. He was frugal, often saving his earnings, and had a profound love for books. His generosity shone through as he frequently shared his literary finds with us, enriching our lives with knowledge. My oldest son also excelled in his career by serving as a role model for his siblings by joining the military. His decision set a standard of bravery and responsibility, leaving a lasting impact on his brothers. He chose not to return home after his service, embracing a life of independence. A colleague once remarked to me that he had already grown into a man of character before he even left our home. I hold immense pride in all my children, each carving their own distinct paths in life.

When I was a preteen, my father shared a piece of advice with me in the kitchen. At a time when the idea of children of a husband or a good man was far from my mind. He said, "Molly, you won't find a good man in this city; you'll have to head south." Reflecting on his words now, at my current age, I see them in a new light. To convey his sentiment more clearly: my father loved us dearly and had his own unique way of expressing it. He did not elaborate on his "milk and the cow" analogy, but what he meant was "Daughter, be patient and venture south to find your husband, because the prospects here in this city are quite limited." Even today reflecting on my beloved father statement "Why would a father tell his daughter about a man?" you may ask. Most parents tell their children to venture out to find a career and go to college. My guess, to elaborate, is that my father was being realistic. There was no fund for college; he saw his daughter married with a good man one day, and that was his way his true way of a daughter's blessing from him; he knew that women need a source of protection. And of course, the South is vast. In this chapter I am not displaying an offer for a date. This is an example of a father's love for her daughter, and not just in pursuit of a career for independence, as the world has instructed women in America.

The fathers of my sons are not the only influential men in my life. There was also a minister who, upon seeking my pastor's approval, expressed a desire to marry me. Looking back, I recognize a period of promiscuity in my life, spanning from age eighteen to twenty. This reflection recalls the power of parental influence. Like Isaac from the Bible, who blessed his children, parents should be conscious of their impact. The way we perceive, speak to, and speak about our children is pivotal. It is equally important to be vigilant about their exposure to social media and the internet. Actively engaging with their world, meeting their teachers, and carefully selecting babysitters is crucial for their well-being. Despite my deep respect for teachers and the challenges they face, it is necessary to stay alert. Unfortunately, there have been instances in the news where teachers have crossed boundaries with students."

CHAPTER 19

A Child's Value and Learning

Reflecting on desire, I have contemplated the distinction: Is it merely about physical intimacy, or is it about finding a genuine, loving partner? Human nature inherently includes a desire for sexual relationships. However, engaging in such relationships carries responsibilities and potential consequences. The choice of a partner should be considered carefully. I trust that, upon sincere request, divine guidance can lead one to the right person. This journey often transforms pain into purpose, marking the true difference.

There is a saying that acquiring physical intimacy is easier than obtaining food. However, offering such intimacy does not ensure a lasting or committed relationship. My advice, particularly to women, is to be discerning in your relationships. If you are seeking more than just a physical connection, it's crucial to protect yourself from being perceived solely as an object of desire. The commitment of marriage is never guaranteed by physical intimacy alone.

In the past, explicit content was restricted to adult-only venues like strip clubs or adult theaters. Now, the digital age has made it possible for anyone, from children to adults, to access or even share revealing images on social media. This widespread exposure raises concerns about privacy and the implications of sharing such personal content with the world.

When individuals, especially women, reveal too much on social media, it leaves little to the imagination and can negatively affect meaningful relationships. Such overexposure can lead to one partner fantasizing about strangers they see in photos, diverting their attention and thoughts away from their significant other. This can foster perverse thoughts and behaviors.

The saying, "Blessed are the pure in heart, for they shall see God," suggests that purity of heart allows one to perceive God's presence and work in their relationships. The belief that "all things work together for the good for those who love and are called according to His purpose" implies that divine guidance plays a role in shaping one's life and relationships. When people expose themselves on social media, it often indicates a search for attention rather than a specific person or meaningful connection.

We are often encouraged to be independent women, acquiring our own car, home, and possessions, fostering the belief that we do not need a man. However, through personal growth and observation, I have come to understand that a woman managing everything alone—be it buying a home, paying for her car, funding her education, or even raising children—can sometimes become hardened or bitter. I do not believe it's wrong to achieve these things independently. Yet, there is a realization that comes with age. A woman who has single-handedly accumulated all this, without a partner's support, may find herself physically and emotionally worn down, potentially neglecting her own well-being in the process.

In my observations of Kevin Samuels's videos, he often posed two questions to women: their dress size (notably not their pants size, emphasizing a distinction between men and women) and their weight. His commentary, especially directed toward many Black women, was that they are generally overweight. This brings to light another aspect: the elevated expectations women often have regarding a man's income, especially when seeking a "high value" man, while sometimes falling short in their own contributions.

To align with the concept of a "high value" woman also, it is suggested to move beyond the idea of using sex rarely proves a secure relationship. This approach rarely proves effective, as there are many women will choose to pursue this path. My message is particularly for women who place high value on themselves not in the form things and beauty but personal respect to themselves.

Reflecting on our choices within our communities, especially in Black communities, there's a tendency to settle for certain types of men—like the "dope dealer" without a stable job, or someone with any job, thinking that it's sufficient if he's employed. This contrasts with certain cultures where young women are groomed to find men capable of providing for them. In contrast, American culture often promotes a "do as thou wilt" attitude, which can lead to a lack of accountability for our actions.

This highlights the importance of self-awareness and thoughtful decision making in our relationships:

Embracing independence does not mean disregarding the wisdom of responsible men in our lives. In fact, it is a powerful step to involve your father or a respected male figure in your relationship choices, if possible. My daughter-in-law set a wonderful example; she insisted my son seek her father's blessing. This act of respect is often missing in relationships, particularly in Black culture, leading to challenges. The biblical story of Ruth and Boaz illustrates the virtue of patience and seeking a partner who respects not just you, but also your family's wisdom. Remember, a man often understands another man's intentions clearly. If your father is no longer with us, a trusted male relative who genuinely cares for you can offer invaluable insight. Their guidance can be a beacon, helping you navigate the complexities of relationships with confidence and clarity.

I want to share an important piece of advice: if you are developing feelings for someone but notice warning signs in the relationship, it's vital to refrain from becoming physically intimate. The reason is that human beings are naturally inclined to form deep emotional connections through physical touch. This can lead to a feeling of deep obligation towards your partner, making it challenging to leave, even in unhealthy situations. This difficulty in leaving is often seen in cases of women trapped in abusive relationships, unable to break free due to the bond formed through intimacy. My own experience is a testament to this. I was in a marriage filled with red flags for nearly five years. It reached a point where he expelled me from our home with harsh words. That day, I left with my four children and had no choice but to move into my mother's small, seven hundred-square-foot, one-bedroom apartment in a senior living facility. This personal ordeal underscores the importance of heeding early warning signs in a relationship and the impact of physical intimacy on our ability to make healthy decisions.

During my journey as a single mother, I received incredible support from those around me, including generous donations like cars. My supervisor once gave me a car when my children were still in school, two in high school and two in elementary. Another car was a kind gift from a church member. I recall a time when I was at Walmart to get a tire changed, and the tire blew out while my sons were in the car with me. Thankfully, my father had taught me essential car maintenance skills, like changing a tire, especially in an era when cell phones were not as common as they are now. Back then, owning a cell phone was a sign of high status. He also taught me how to add fluid to cars. As a single mother, it is crucial to have a broad range of skills. Unfortunately, I once experienced an engine lock-up in one of those cars because I had not checked the oil—a mistake I never repeated. Through all these challenges, my parents were my steadfast support until they fell ill and passed away.

CHAPTER 20

The Impact of Your Life on Your Children

As a single mom, I made the conscious decision to raise my children without a man in the household, though I recognize the importance of having two parents. The ideal scenario for a child is to be nurtured by both a mother and a father. My sons, with an age gap of eight to ten years between them, faced their own challenges due to our family structure. After my divorce, when my youngest son was only two and the third son was three, my two eldest sons, aged eleven and twelve, had to shoulder significant responsibilities. This was the situation when I had to leave our home. At the time, I was about to turn thirty.

Every morning, the two eldest would walk a block to take their younger brothers to the childcare center, as my job required me to start early. They then had to trek back to catch the school bus for themselves. This routine was a direct consequence of the lifestyle choices and circumstances I had to navigate. It is a poignant reminder that the decisions of parents, whether willingly or forced by circumstances, can inadvertently impact their children's lives. My sons would even visit me at the hospital where I worked, sitting in the waiting area to have their breakfast. This experience highlights how children often bear the weight of their parents' life choices, even when they are not directly involved. My second son made admirable sacrifices during his time in a local private high school. To support me, he took on jobs at both the school and the nearby Kroger store. He even expressed to the school his desire to help me out. Transportation options were limited then—we relied on city buses or cabs, as services like Uber and Lyft did not exist. Owning a cell phone was a symbol of affluence.

I vividly recall times when I bought bags of lollipops for my son to sell to his classmates, so he could have money for lunch. There were occasions when I had to use my own lunch break to walk from my workplace and bring him meals from the hospital cafeteria. He always said he preferred my lunches over school food, even from a youthful age. This was evident when he went on a school trip and was delighted with the lunch I packed for him. These moments reflect not just the financial struggles we faced, but also the strong bond and mutual support between us during those challenging times.

Life presented many challenges. We stayed with my mother, who lived nearby in senior citizen apartments, until my sister assisted me in securing my own place. Later, my mother faced her own battles with diabetes and cancer. During her illness, she was my main support with my sons, and her absence is deeply felt.

Losing my mother and father has been incredibly hard, yet I understand that sometimes, when suffering becomes too great, it is a release for them to pass on. My mother's pain was so intense in her final days in hospice care that she often cried out for medication to ease her discomfort. These experiences, though heart-wrenching, have taught me about the complexities of life, the strength of family bonds, and the inevitable cycle of life and loss.

CHAPTER 21

Reflecting on My Support System

My father, who lived in a senior citizen apartment across town, was often difficult to reach due to the absence of a phone in his home. He passed away in May 1996. My mother followed, leaving us in February 2001. With their passing, my foundational support system was gone. During this challenging time, I turned to prayer, asking for just enough financial means to care for my sons. I devoted my life to raising them without a partner, without the presence of their father. Now, they have all grown into men, a testament to the journey we have navigated together.

CHAPTER 22

Encouraging Positive Influences for Your Child

Reflecting on current societal trends; concerns how public exposure has evolved. Today, the internet is rife with images of individuals, both women and men, displaying themselves in scant clothing or in compromising positions for attention on various online platforms. This kind of exposure, which was once confined to adult entertainment venues like pornographic videos and strip clubs, accessible only to those aged eighteen and above for a fee, has now permeated the digital landscape. As a result, children and teens with easy access to cell phones and the internet can inadvertently encounter such content. This shift underscores the critical need for parents to be vigilant about their children's online activities and to guide them toward positive and age-appropriate content.

Looking back at a life marked by various mistakes and decisions, a standout memory is of my father, in the kitchen, imparting unexpected advice about men. His words, seemingly sarcastic at the time, made a lasting impression on me, a young and impressionable daughter who wasn't even considering relationships then. Even now, his words resonate with me.

This experience highlights an important lesson for parents: the words you speak to your children linger in their minds. They may not always recall them immediately, but these conversations often resurface, leaving a profound impact. Therefore, it is crucial to speak positively and thoughtfully to them. My father's advice was a caution against the men in our city, suggesting that I would encounter many wrong choices here. He implied that the right man for me would be found elsewhere, specifically in the South. His emphasis was not on the man's wealth, class, religiosity, or godliness, but on his inherent goodness. This profound guidance from my father has stayed with me, a reminder of the power of a parent's words in shaping their child's perspectives and choices. I count this a blessing from my father. His daughter grew up and matured, and with age came wisdom and understanding, with the desire to author a book.

When we talk about someone being "good," we refer to a combination of desirability, suitability for a specific purpose, moral righteousness, and the capacity to provide benefit or advantage. A person embodying "goodness" aligns with these qualities, even those unspoken by my father. This concept of goodness is particularly relevant in the context of the increasing exposure of children and teenagers to explicit content online.

The rampant availability of such content, where individuals, both women and men, publicly display themselves, raises serious concerns about the preservation of innocence. When a child, initially shielded by their parents' teachings about relationships and integrity, encounters free-access pornography, it can profoundly impact their understanding and values. This exposure risks eroding the moral and ethical framework instilled by their parents. Furthermore, it increases the likelihood of the child being subject to molestation or exploitation. In this digital age, it is crucial for parents to be vigilant about their children's online interactions to safeguard their innocence and uphold the values of goodness they strive to instill.

These individuals seeking attention are in pursuit of a relationship. Consider three women: the first is affluently wealthy and promiscuous, while the second, though financially strained, shares similar promiscuous traits. Both are involved intimately with men. Which one might sustain a long-term relationship? The third woman, in contrast, reserves physical intimacy for a committed, marital bond and seeks consent from her father. She is also noted for her modest attire. It seems likely that the third woman has a better prospect for a lasting relationship.

It is often said that men are like hunters, and when a woman is too readily available without any commitment, she does not present a challenge to pursue. On the other hand, a woman who says, "No, ask my father. I will not give myself to you without boundaries" will prompt a man to make a choice. He may either walk away or stay and commit, aligning with the virtuous woman described in Proverbs chapter 31: 10 Who can find a virtuous woman? for her price is far above rubies. The third woman embodies the ideal mentioned in Proverbs 18:22: "He who finds a wife finds a good thing." This reflects the virtue highlighted in Proverbs 31 starting with verse ten to be read through verse 31. This book aims to enlighten its readers, encouraging them to view their children as precious beings deserving of protection, love, and guidance, thereby positively shaping the future.

CHAPTER 23

A Lesson in Integrity

The concept of suffering leading to righteousness is profound. Suffering entails experiencing pain, distress, or hardship, while righteousness is about being morally right or just. When suffering not expressing sicknesses or diseases in the body. But relating to integrity (honesty) I am expressing chastity in a world where pleasure is more loved than waiting. Suffering is also clearly stated as hurting in want of something that women in general long for and that is the love of a man when emotions are involved especially when two families also are affected. In reflecting on this, it becomes apparent that women's primary gift to men is respect. Women are partners and supporters, not caretakers or just objects for men's desires. Even a woman with immense wealth loses her essence if she compromises her integrity, which is defined as honesty and strong moral principles. This loss translates to a diminishing of her moral value, her soul, and her self-worth. One might ponder her standing in the eyes of God and who truly makes the decisions in life.

God can guide our choices by granting the desires of our heart or responding to our prayers, which is often the best path. However, when we ask for guidance, it is crucial to ensure our desires align with God's will. The decision is ours. Like choosing a flower from a garden, a man makes his choice thoughtfully.

On another note, a woman's financial status does not dictate her actions. A wealthy woman might still engage in casual relationships, just as a woman with little means might do the same. Similarly, a jobholder, regardless of her job's pay grade, can find herself in similar situations. Yet, there exists a woman who seeks something more meaningful. She desires a man she can respect, understanding the true value of a relationship, one she never experienced or one she lost. She recognizes that respect and love are fundamental, envisioning a partnership where the man is the provider, and she is the supportive partner. This is the essence of their relationship.

Reflecting on Ways a Woman Can Support a Man She Admires While Maintaining Integrity:

1. Express interest and support his career endeavors.
2. Practice gratitude and appreciation.
3. Reserve physical intimacy for a committed, meaningful relationship.
4. Communicate concisely and effectively.
5. Be thoughtful and distinguish yourself positively.
6. Maintain your own identity, which in turn helps you respect him as a man. Sharing this approach can be profoundly impactful.
7. Be open to external advice in professional matters but prioritize seeking guidance from God.
8. Consider the significance of the number eight, symbolizing new beginnings, new orders, and rebirth. In this context, remember the essential convergence of love and respect in a relationship.

CHAPTER 24

The Importance of Teaching Your Child—Unveiling Truth

Let's explore misconceptions rooted in childhood experiences and beliefs. I grew up believing that physical contact was essential to maintain a relationship with someone you are attracted to. This belief, however, is far from the truth and can be detrimental to forming meaningful connections. Such a mindset obscures the crucial aspects you need to see in a person, like their spirit or character, their kindness or selfishness.

Currently, I know someone whom others might hastily judge as selfish or cheap. However, by being a good listener and delving deeper, I discovered his frugality and conservatism, which is often mistaken for stinginess. It's a reminder that when people are well off, others might assume they are extravagant.

The key message here is the importance of genuinely understanding someone. Without taking the time to know each other, outsiders or a different sex may be perceived as threats. This chapter underscores the significance of teaching your child to look beyond surface-level judgments and seek deeper understanding in relationships.

Learning life's lessons can be challenging, especially when important advice is not imparted early on. To a child, understanding the importance of personal boundaries is crucial, but often this guidance is overlooked due to the perception of children as young and impressionable.

At twenty-nine, an age often considered a woman's prime, I found myself introspective and concerned about my desirability as a mother of four, raising them alone. This period marked a significant turning point in my life, drawing me closer to God and leading me to seek guidance in prayer.

A profound realization emerged about my lifelong belief that intimacy was the way to win a man's affection—a belief I now recognize as a flawed misconception. Such a mindset is destructive for anyone, man, or woman. At twenty-nine, I made a conscious decision to avoid further pregnancies and to step away from relationships. This choice made me no different from a teenager who finds herself a single mother—both of us navigating life's complexities and learning from our experiences.

In today's societal dynamics, I have observed a trend where men often prioritize physical intimacy over respect in relationships. This contrasts with the biblical principle where men are typically seen as the loving party and women as the respectful one. When a woman genuinely loves a man, it represents an extraordinary dynamic. In such a scenario, a woman might put earnest effort into her appearance and actions to capture his attention, emphasizing her role as a good listener and supportive partner.

However, if a man insists on physical intimacy as a prerequisite, it can fundamentally alter the relationship's dynamics.

This shift may impact the mutual understanding and respect that should ideally form the foundation of a loving, long-term partnership.

CHAPTER 25

Discovering the Secret to Sustaining Love

On my journey, I uncovered a vital secret to maintaining love: the necessity of spiritual resilience and prayer. It was a revelation to me that love involves a kind of spiritual warfare, one that requires prayer and sometimes fasting. There are countless forces that challenge our spirit, tempting us to surrender and abandon our efforts. This crucial aspect of sustaining love was something I had to discover on my own. It is a key reason why many people struggle with, or give up on, nurturing and preserving love in their relationships. Love, as I have learned, is indeed a fight—a fight that requires spiritual strength and dedication.

The Depth of a Woman's Love

When a woman loves a man genuinely, it is akin to him discovering a treasure trove. Her love transcends physical attraction, and she dedicates herself to nurturing this love. Such a woman waits for the right moment for intimacy, a decision made jointly when they both feel their love has deepened sufficiently. It is rare to find women who prioritize emotional connection and love before embarking on a physical relationship, and I proudly belong to this category. This stance is not about casual encounters or mere physical proximity; it's about a deep, heartfelt bond.

In my life, I have had opportunities to develop relationships with men, including one I've known since childhood, yet I chose not to pursue physical intimacy without an underlying emotional connection. My professional life, too, is filled with interactions with men, but without the requisite emotional bond, my desire for physical intimacy has not been kindled. There was one exception, but that relationship did not evolve into physical intimacy, and I view this as a positive outcome. This reflects my firm belief in the importance of a meaningful emotional connection as the foundation for any deeper relationship.

In today's world, some women engage in relationships based on superficial attributes like looks or financial status, rather than genuine love. Reflecting on the virtuous woman described in the Bible, it is clear that such a woman encompasses even more than what is written.

"Traits of a Virtuous Woman"

1. She reveres, honors, and respects God and His teachings.
2. She does not trivialize intimacy.
3. Her loyalty to her partner is unwavering.
4. She shows deep respect for her man.
5. Her support for her partner is steadfast.
6. She fosters a balanced relationship and avoids mind games.
7. Her prayers are often for her partner's well-being.
8. Hardworking and initiative-taking, she is always willing to contribute.
9. She cultivates an environment filled with love and peace.

10. She refrains from criticizing her partner.
11. She is a source of motivation and encouragement.
12. She does not try to outdo or compete with her man.

This ultimate point resonates with me. Many women, including myself, often feel the need to compete with men. As a single mother, I experienced the challenges of managing stress and the responsibility of a family. It led to personal neglect, a common issue for many women in similar situations. Yet I am grateful for the strength God gave me. This journey has taught me the importance of partnership, of being a supportive companion to a man, not just bearing burdens alone. A virtuous woman, as I have learned, is both strong in her own right and a pillar of support in her relationship.

CHAPTER 26

Guiding Your Daughter to Embrace Womanhood

D elving deeper into the concept of a virtuous woman, it is clear she is distinct in her ways, and her husband is aware of this. Her commitment is unwavering, devoted solely to her husband. While many women strive for godliness and seek forgiveness, this woman is distinguished by the trust her husband places in her. She works diligently, contributing significantly with her efforts. Her value is not just in her wealth but also in her generosity toward the less fortunate.

Her interactions are marked by kindness and wisdom, and her attire, while elegant, is not intended to attract undue attention or portray a false image. Her dress code honors God, reflecting modesty and respect. This woman's focus is on her own household, not seeking to intrude into others' Above all, her life and actions are guided by a deep reverence for God, setting a moral and spiritual example for her family. She embodies the virtues that any parent would hope to instill in their daughter, demonstrating that true womanhood is defined by character, integrity, and a heart aligned with divine principles.

CHAPTER 27

Fostering Mutual Respect from Childhood

In my life's journey, I have come to understand an essential aspect of personal growth. I refer to a certain individual as a friend, whom I follow on a YouTube channel. My support for this channel is shown through likes, heart emojis or some other form that of a smiling face, comments, and by subscribing for regular updates. Each new video he posts offers insights and learning opportunities. His channel focuses on teaching viewers to build wealth in numerous ways, aiming for financial freedom to enjoy what truly matters in life.

This engagement led me to a realization about relationship building, especially with the opposite sex. Like many others, I noticed that we often are not formally taught how to develop and maintain healthy relationships. This gap in our learning underscores the importance of teaching children about respect and positive interaction from an early age, laying the foundation for successful, respectful relationships in adulthood. Through such early education, we can better understand and navigate the complexities of human connections.

You might be questioning how this relates to the transition from childhood through teenage years to becoming a responsible adult. A key lesson that is often missed is learning to maintain harmonious and respectful relationships with people of the opposite gender, regardless of personal feelings. It is a common misconception that if you have feelings for someone, these emotions must be immediately expressed and acknowledged. However, the reality is that the other person may not reciprocate those feelings.

This led me to a critical decision recently. While following a man's YouTube channel for advice on wealth building, I was confronted with a choice: should I concentrate on the valuable information he was providing, or should I allow my personal feelings to interfere? I chose to focus on the content of his channel, gaining valuable knowledge that transcended mere emotional responses. This decision emphasizes the importance of managing emotions in interactions with others, a vital skill for personal growth and the development of mature, healthy relationships.

Feeling hurt and shedding tears over this experience was a natural response, especially since the topic was wealth-building, not forming relationships with viewers. As women, we often navigate a sea of emotions, and it is crucial to learn how to control them before they begin to control us. Our thoughts can sometimes lead us astray, creating delusions and imaginary scenarios that are far from reality.

This situation teaches an important lesson about opposite-gender relationships: they do not necessarily imply physical contact or emotional attachment. It is essential to recognize that not everyone will reciprocate feelings, and attraction is often to what truly resonates with us. As we age, our appreciation for relationships with family and friends deepens, along with the value we place on our time.

I hope this book will inspire a change in parenting perspectives, encouraging parents to see beyond their children's immediate, tangible needs. Parenting is a serious responsibility. It involves understanding and being actively involved in the complex world children navigate, helping them grow into well-rounded, emotionally intelligent adults.

Milton Keynes UK
Ingram Content Group UK Ltd.
UKHW051857140624
444031UK00017B/205/J